STANDING AT THE THRESHOLD OF DESTINY

Lessons From The Daughters of Zelophehad

HELEN I. HOPKINS

Standing at the Threshold of Destiny:
Lessons from the Daughters of Zelophehad
© February 2020
By Helen I. Hopkins

Editing by Stephanie Montgomery, Unique Communications Concepts
Published in the United States of America by
ChosenButterflyPublishing LLC

 www.cb-publishing.com
All rights reserved under International Copyright Law. Contents and/or cover may not be reproduced, distributed, or transmitted in any form or by any means or stored in a database or retrieval system, without the prior written consent of the publisher and/or authors.

All Scripture quotations, unless otherwise indicated, are taken from the Holy Bible, KING JAMES VERSION (KJV): KING JAMES VERSION, public domain.

Scripture quotations marked AMPC have been taken from the Amplified® Bible (AMPC), Copyright © 1954, 1958, 1962, 1964, 1965, 1987 by The Lockman Foundation. Used by permission. www.Lockman.org

Scriptures marked ESV are from The ESV® Bible (The Holy Bible, English Standard Version®), copyright © 2001 by Crossway, a publishing ministry of Good News Publishers. Used by permission. All rights reserved.

Scripture marked ISV has been taken from the Holy Bible: International Standard Version® Release 2.0. Copyright © 1996-2013 by the ISV Foundation. Used by permission of Davidson Press, LLC. ALL RIGHTS RESERVED INTERNATIONALLY.

Scriptures marked MGG have been taken from The Message Bible. Copyright Â© 1993, 1994, 1995, 1996, 2000, 2001, 2002. Used by permission of NavPress Publishing Group.

Scripture quotations marked (NIV) are taken from the Holy Bible, New International Version®, NIV®. Copyryght © 1973, 1978, 1984, 2011 by Biblica, Inc.™ Used by permission of Zondervan. All rights reserved worldwide. www.zondervan.comThe "NIV" and "New International Version" are trademarks registered in the United States Patent and Trademark Office by Biblica, Inc.™

Scriptures marked NRSV are from Revised Standard Version of the Bible, copyright © 1946, 1952, and 1971 National Council of the Churches of Christ in the United States of America. Used by permission. All rights reserved worldwide.

Scripture quotations marked (TLB) are taken from The Living Bible copyright © 1971. Used by permission of Tyndale House Publishers, a Division of Tyndale House Ministries, Carol Stream, Illinois 60188. All rights reserved.

ISBN: 978-1-945377-09-9
First Edition Printing
Printed in the United States of America
February 2020

STANDING AT THE THRESHOLD OF DESTINY

Endorsements

"I really enjoyed reading your book. I love how you expounded on the daughters (of Zelophehad) and how they related to our lives. I definitely learned some new things. Your heart and soul are felt in the book."

Author Gina Edwards

"There is a very heavy anointing on this book! My spirit was encouraged just from reading the introduction. Encouragement exuded from the words and leaped off the page!"

Dr. Hope Watts
Family Practitioner

"What a blessing! This is a revelation and brought deep insight into a passage of scripture that has been overlooked by most of us. The Study, Reflections and Affirmations are Practical, Inspirational and On Point for this time in our culture and community. Helen has constructed a bridge between the stories of Joseph, Ruth, Gomer, the Daughters of Zelophehad and her own personal testimony - and simultaneously provided a step-by-step guide to achieving our Divine Destiny in Jesus Christ. Thank you for this precious gift!"

Michelle Jacobs Greene

Dedication

This book is dedicated to the courageous women who have determined not to allow their past, present or other painful circumstances dictate their outcome in life. It is also dedicated to my incredible husband, who has always seen the best in me and fuels my ambitions. He stimulates me to reach my highest potential.

Acknowledgements & Thanks:

Special thanks to Denise Yearian who inspired me to write and offered excellent advice and priceless pointers. To Dr. Hope Watts who provided reassurance, valuable feedback and prayers. To Pastor Jacquelyne Parker, who provided administrative support, enthusiasm and timely encouragement. To my Goddaughter, Stephanie Lewis, for lending her professional editing and writing skills and for connecting me with a prestigious publishing company. And to my children, who have always challenged me to excel in life. I am most thankful to God who spoke to me several years ago saying, *"there's a book inside you."* To Him be all Glory.

Contents

Endorsements v

Dedication vi

Acknowledgements & Thanks: vii

Foreword xi

    CHAPTER 1: Introduction 1

    CHAPTER 2: Breaking the Taskmasters Bonds 3

    CHAPTER 3: Dare to Dream 17

    CHAPTER 4: "The Apple of the Eye" 31

    CHAPTER 5: Causing to Forget 45

    CHAPTER 6: Our Beginning Does Not Determine Our End 57

    CHAPTER 7: A Rock in a Hard Place 73

    CHAPTER 8: A Crown of Glory & A Royal Diadem 85

    CHAPTER 9: Five is the number of Grace 99

    CHAPTER 10: A Gateway of Hope 113

    CHAPTER 11: A New Mindset 125

    CHAPTER 12: Treasures of Darkness 139

    CHAPTER 13: Living Your Legacy 149

Practical Application Page 161

About the Author 167

Foreword

Wow! What a word in due season. Helen encourages, exhorts, exposes, elevates, liberates and delivers as she shares with us the truth that no matter what family you are born into or other opposing conditions, God has a plan and a purpose for your life. Helen reminds us that sometimes we may feel defined by life's circumstances, but we need to remember that each of us have a destiny to fulfill. It is not our external value that determines it. She assures us that no person, or demeaning words that was ever spoken over our lives in the past has the power to hold us back from becoming the person God wants us to be or fulfilling the plan that God has for our lives. Helen shares with us how to stand firm in who we are in Christ and to take our rightful place. She also tells us how to receive our inheritance and to fulfill that which the lord has purposed for each one of our lives.

As you read the contents of this book, you will discover how to break the taskmaster's bonds that try to stop, abort and or annihilate our dreams. We are told how special and precious we are in the sight of God and that we are the Apple of His Eye - and to know that we are Fearfully and Wonderfully Made. We are Graced for whatever we face.

Pastor Mary Cooper
Founder of Daughters of Esther

INTRODUCTION

Standing at the Threshold of Destiny

This book is inspired by the story of an Old Testament father named Zelophehad and his five daughters. It will encourage you to put the past behind you, break free from your present limitations, redefine who you are in Christ and pursue the amazing destiny that God has in store for you.

The account of this father's personal battle and the ultimate triumph of these five daughters will inspire you to have hope in the midst of whatever adversity you are facing. It will help eliminate fears resulting from past hurts, pains, rejections and failures. You will gain a positive expectation for good concerning your days ahead.

You will become invigorated to resurrect your buried potential, misdirected goals and misplaced aspirations. You will feel inspired to reclaim your ambition in life. You will come to realize that your past does not define you nor does it determine your destinations.

This book is designed to help you develop an unwavering faith amid the storms of life and to trust the Lord completely when dealing with opposition. It will fortify you with renewed strength as you discover who you are in Christ, so that you can out last life's adversities.

Many of us are standing at the threshold of destiny, but continuously face what seems like impossible or insurmountable odds. You will be inspired to step over the threshold of destiny and move forward with confidence and courage to discover and fulfill your own God-given purpose and receive the inheritance established for you through Jesus Christ.

This book will leave you enlightened, enthused and astonished. You will discover what God says about you and come to trust that He has a plan for you far beyond your highest expectations

The message will lift your spirit and enhance your self-image as you discover that your identity does not come from personal wealth, accomplishments or successes in life. Neither are you defined by the negative words of declaration over you or harsh treatment toward you. Your identity is found solely in Christ; you are

defined by who He says you are. Your past does not determine your destiny, your present circumstances do not dictate your potential and neither do hurts, pains and failures characterize you. You are standing at the threshold of your destiny.

CHAPTER ONE

Breaking the Taskmasters Bonds

This story is a narrative about a father and his five daughters who lived during Old Testament times found in the Book of

NUMBERS, CHAPTERS 26 AND 27.

Most of us have experienced hardships, which sometimes leave us feeling flawed in our character or personality. Viewed as damaged goods, we've been labeled as weak, rubbish and irrelevant.

Our present circumstances sometimes make us feel limited, confined and without potential. It feels as if we are stuck and unable to move forward in life. It appears that our very existence is hanging in limbo or in an agonizing, indeterminate state.

Sadly, we often define ourselves by our past and through the reflections or images we have of ourselves that result from debilitating experiences or from unkind words others have spoken over us. We lack confidence, practice self-doubt, self-loathing and self-criticism.

Have you ever felt like you did not fit in or measure up to other's expectations? Were you sometimes made to feel inferior because of uncontrollable circumstances? Perhaps you did not complete your education, or you suffered an early pregnancy, a divorce, rape, incest, abandonment, rejection or you encountered some other form of abuse, neglect, sarcastic or disrespectful behavior that made you feel insignificant.

Some of you have had bad things happen to you that were of no fault of your own. These atrocities left you devastated and overwhelmed.

It is Time You Regain Your Sense of Worth.

Discover your value and significance. Take back your life and move forward. Reclaim your destiny!

As you read about the daughters of Zelophehad, you will see that you are not alone.

None of these things have the power to condemn you to the past unless you permit them. You are not defined by the negative things committed or experienced in the past - including the wrong decisions, the opposing opinions of others or the failures of lineages before you.

God Has Not Forgotten You

You are created to be celebrated - not mishandled or tolerated. This story about the daughters of Zelophehad will help you no longer see yourself through the distorted reflection portrayed by your painful past or by the mistreatment of others, but through the mirror of God's word.

Like these five daughters, many men and women have suffered various kinds of devastating situations and have struggled to overcome their past. They fought hard to reverse or conquer their former conditions in order to get where they are today.

In earlier times, women had to combat discrimination in society just because they were born female. Many women could not find adequate employment, develop a career, enter into ministry or further their education. For many years, a woman could not achieve the same level of success or obtain the same salary as a man for performing identical tasks. This struggle remains part of the fabric of our society even today. While there has been some degree of progress, the battle continues to rage on as women strive to obtain recognition in various cultures.

You need to know that God has not forgotten you. He will open the doors of opportunity for you to fulfill the dreams and visions that 'He' put in your heart. His love for you is the same yesterday, today and forever. He is unchangeable and not limited by the laws of the land, financial restrictions, educational dysfunction, physical disabilities, ethnicity or cultural prejudices, family history or other barriers and obstructions.

As you continue reading, you will discover the definition of the names of Zelophehad and each of his five daughters. As you discover these amazing definitions, you will experience the unfolding of a compelling story that is astoundingly beautiful and informative.

This Father Suffered Personal Struggles Yet Produced Five Phenomenal Daughters

These daughters thrived under difficult and challenging circumstances.

They resisted injustice in society and excelled in a man's world, all while developing and maintaining a positive self-image and self-esteem.

In the midst of all this, God took them through a process to bring them out of obscurity and into a glorious finale. You will be astonished as you witness the overwhelming power of God to take such common lives and use them in extraordinary and incredible fashion.

I want to introduce you to the patriarchal character in this story:

He is the father of the five extraordinary daughters whom you will later meet. As already mentioned, his name is Zelophehad.

His name means;'Shadow of Fear'.

The daughters of Zelophehad grew up under the obstacles associated with the shadow of fear that hovered over their father like a dark cloud on a gloomy day.

History tells us: "The Israelites were made to serve the Egyptians with rigor"

As a small boy, Zelophehad most likely grew up under the watchful eyes of the Egyptian taskmasters. Serving the Egyptians with 'rigor' indicates they were required to be painstakingly meticulous, utterly thorough and precise, giving detailed attention to every task. Zelophehad may have served under their harsh control as a young man.

Zelophehad's youthful eyes most likely witnessed the cruel acts and the harsh treatment his people suffered. He probably witnessed the heartbreak of the families who lost loved ones due to the heartless and brutal demands of these overseers. The cries of the people were heard daily and their prayers went up like smoke before God fervently.

Many of us as believers are suffering under the cruel control of the taskmasters of today. We do not like to think of ourselves as slaves to anything. Nevertheless; if we are controlled by ungodly cravings, overwhelming lusts, addictive behaviors, unnatural desires, ungodly influences, bondages or other strongholds - then we are a slave to these things. These include wicked mindsets, attitudes, opinions, wrong perceptions and other self-condemning beliefs and evil governances.

Zelophehad came out of Egypt, but was still a slave to fear. He had a 'slave mentality' that his new geographical locality alone could not break. Fear dominated and controlled his life like a haunting silhouette.

Many of us struggle with mental, physical and emotional taskmasters. We must ask God to reveal and uproot the taskmasters of our mind, our will and our emotions.

Interestingly, the bible tells us that; *"The more these taskmasters afflicted them, the more they grew"*.

The Israelites were more and mightier than the Egyptians and so the Egyptians feared that if war were to break out, the Israelites would join their enemies and overtake them. Thus, they put them in fetters and made them their slaves.

I love the statement; *"The more they afflicted them, the more they grew."*

What the enemy intended to destroy them only made them stronger. Though they served the Egyptians with 'rigor' (difficulty, trouble, hardship and restriction); God equally and more rigorously (thoroughly and systematically) broke their bonds and set them free.

Egypt represents bondage. This lets me know that we too can come out of our bondages, strongholds, addictions, afflictions and hardships of life better, stronger, more fully capable and wiser.

We do not have to break under the weight of our wretched past or the circumstances of our present day. Instead, through Christ we can rise up victorious and emerge triumphant.

From Deliverance to Destiny

In the Second Book of Moses called *"Exodus"* (Deliverance), God raised up a deliverer (One sent to free someone from slavery or other such forms of bondage). After many years, God heard their cries and gave them a deliverer.

He hears our cries as well and will deliver us from the taskmaster's bonds.

God sent Moses to tell Pharaoh to *"Let My People Go"*. However, Pharaoh's heart was hardened.

God sent various plagues; water became blood, frogs and lice swarmed Egypt and livestock of Egypt died. There were also plagues of boils and hail, locust and thick darkness and eventually the death of Egypt's firstborn.

Whenever God brings you out of something, He is bringing you out from the old thing to bring you into the new thing that He has for you.

God did not simply say to Pharaoh, *"Let My People Go!"* He followed this statement by saying *"So that they may worship Me"*. You were not designed to serve taskmasters. The reason for your creation was so that you could have a personal relationship with God through Christ and serve Him only.

God Always Provides a 'Deliverer'

Pharaoh finally released the Hebrew slaves and they crossed over into the wilderness (on dry ground), by way of the divided Red Sea. I cannot imagine what it must have felt like for them to walk through the Red Sea on dry ground with elevated walls of water as high as they could see on their right and their left. All the while, they were watching a dividing path appear right before them, providing clear passage.

In addition, the enemy was behind them in hot pursuit. However, God destroyed their enemies as the walls of water came crashing down on them.

When God unshackles you from the taskmasters, He will destroy their control so that they can no longer pursue you. They will no longer dominate, manipulate or control your life. Their chains are broken, nullified and destroyed.

The Israelites crossed safely to their destiny. Celebration broke out in this new place. However, what should have been an eleven-day journey in this barren region became forty long years.

Moses, whose name means 'savior' and 'drawn out of the water', led the Israelites out of Egypt, escaping the wrath of the Egyptian soldiers. It's interesting that Moses - who was 'drawn out of the water', was chosen by God to deliver (rescue, liberate) the Israelites *"through"* or *"by means of"* the water.

Not only did He bring them out - they emerged loaded with the wealth of Egypt.

It is here (just before coming out of the wilderness), that we pick up the story of the daughters of Zelophehad.

The bible does not tell us the specifics, but the daughters of Zelophehad were most likely conceived during the 40-year escapade.

It was at the end of their journey when the leaders called the families together for the distribution of inheritance. Many fathers - including Zelophehad, died and the sons were now standing in line awaiting their rightful distribution.

Many births and deaths took place in the wilderness and a census was taken in order to number the families (Numbers 26). It is noteworthy that only the 'sons' of the families were called to come and stand before Moses, Eleazar the priest, the leaders and the entire congregation for distribution of inheritance according to the laws. The women were not included.

Abruptly an uncommon thing occurred. Chapter 27, verse 1; *"Then came the daughters of Zelophehad..."* (KJV)

Our Up-Bringing Does Not Determine Our Destiny

Zelophehad's daughters played a key role in this distribution, which you will see in subsequent chapters.

Before disclosing the daughter's magnificent story, I want to further lay a foundation so that you will better understand the occurrences that brought these women to a place of prominence in biblical history.

We are all, to some degree, products of our environment and upbringing; however, as adults and as followers of Christ, we have the responsibility to choose who we wish to become and how we wish to live our lives in accordance with God's plan.

Contrary to popular belief, we are not 'destined' to repeat the history of our family members or ancestors; instead, we have a destiny that was pre-ordained by our creator and His plans for us are for our good and not for evil.

Zelophehad eventually broke the power of fear and its control from his life - but not before considerable harm was done to his first two daughters, as we will see when we discover the meaning of each of his daughter's names.

As Zelophehad began to live life in this brand-new freedom, he empowered his daughters to live free from fear and they went on to eventually fulfill their divine destiny and to influence the lives of many women. It is an empowering revelation to grasp the limitless and overwhelming ability a father has over his children. It is no wonder the enemy loves to destroy families, marriages and households through division, strife and the breaking of the marriage covenant.

The Significance of the Father

The original root word for 'husband' is 'house-band'. This in itself tells us the importance of a husband and father's role in the family. The world is full of children who have no sense of direction or purpose in their life because they grew up without a father. They are exposed to the dangers and destructive powers this world possesses because the 'house-band' has been removed.

The Value of a Father's Presence Must Never Be Undermined

Many children seek to fill their need for acceptance and validation by joining gangs or other cliques in order to gain a sense of family or brotherhood.

Many daughters give themselves to the first male who declares, "*I love you*" because they long for the validation and approval they did not receive from a father.

House-band is a two-part or compound word:

The word 'House' means: household, family, community and dynasty.

'Band' means belt or secure.

The husband's role therefore, is to hold the family together cohesively and to provide a sense of significance, safety and security.

Interestingly, the Hebrew definition for 'Son' is 'Ben' which means "*a builder of the family; appointed to; worthy.*"

This is why they felt it was so significant for men to bear sons in those days. Every father wanted to leave behind 'a builder of the family dynasty'.

He was appointed to carry on the father's name - unlike daughters, who took on the surname of their husband upon marriage.

Many sons who grow up in absentee father homes will grow up to become husbands and fathers. However, when the 'house-band' (husband/father) is not present, the son has no example or role model to show him how to be a builder of the family. He lacks instruction and direction. Even absent fathers can positively impact their children's lives by maintaining a healthy relationship with them outside the home.

I wish to God that men would understand the inspiring gift, the treasure, the value that they are to the family. Absent fathers have successfully influenced their children, despite opposing circumstances, when developing amicable relationships with the mother. Still, it will require a two-part sacrifice.

Even so, only the knowledge of God's unconditional love and acceptance has the power to counteract the pain, heal the fragmented lives and fill the void of the absence of an earthly father's love. Many children are left angry and possess violent tendencies because they felt rejected, forsaken or abandoned by their father. There was no father to tell them who they are and to point out their potential.

Eph. 6:4 tells fathers *to be careful not to exasperate (frustrate, irritate, enrage), their children. They are to bring them up in the training (preparation, teaching, guidance, coaching), and instruction (tutoring, lessons, command), of the Lord – by direction and by example.*

Arrows in the Hand of a Warrior

Psalm 127:4 points out that, children are like arrows in the hands of a warrior. They are sent forth like rockets or missiles to aim for a specific goal. Unfortunately, many do not have a feeling of purpose and lack dreams and visions, so they fail to hit a projected target. When a rocket or missile is launched without a focused object in mind, utter destruction is the result. A father has the ability to provide such a mark by teaching his children how to discover their purpose and by igniting a fire of ambition. If the father is the bow and the children are his arrows, it goes without saying that it is God who is the archer. An 'archer' is one who is perceptive, knowing, intentional and calculating. The child is in the hand of the father, but the father must place himself in the hand of God to fulfill his fatherly assignments.

Children need fathers who will 'war' for them and 'point' their lives like arrows, in a positive direction. By warring for them he stands in the gap, prayerfully and naturally, between them and any conflict or struggles they face. He fights to give them a secure environment, the best education and generally provide all their needs. His love, encouragement and affirmations are vital in positioning them to become the men and women God has purposed them to be.

In bible days, many fathers spoke blessings over their children (Gen. 48:15-16). They laid hands on them and imparted affirmations over their lives, which empowered them for their future and pointed them toward their destiny.

Statistics tell us the children who come from homes where the father is not present are more likely to experience early pregnancies, dabble in drugs and alcohol, drop out of school, join gangs and experience incarceration. (https://www.fatherhood.org/fatherhood-data-statistics)

However, Zelophehad stands as a fatherly example - while we cannot change our history, we can change our destiny and that of our children by simply calling out to God and allowing Him to transform us. Our children do not have to be a statistic.

Reflections

Breaking the Taskmaster's Bond
Chapter One

1). The daughters of Zelophehad grew up under the obstacles associated with the shadow of fear that hovered over their father and initially felt inferior.

> *Have you ever felt like you did not fit in or measure up to the expectations of others? Were you made to feel inferior because of uncontrollable circumstances? How have you overcome?*

2). The Israelites were made to serve the Egyptians with rigor. They suffered much hardship. God sent them a deliverer named Moses. God told Moses to tell Pharaoh to *"let my people go, so that they might serve me."*

> *Jesus came to deliver us from the harsh taskmasters of today. Since giving your heart to Christ, what has He delivered you from so that you might serve God more fully?*

3). You are not defined by the negative things you have done or experienced.

> *Has your past tried to define you? What steps might you take to silence the internal critic and the voice of the enemy?*

4). In our own lives, it seems that the more we are afflicted, the more we grow when we put our trust in God.

How have you grown or become stronger as a result of the afflictions you've suffered?

Scriptural Inheritance Affirmation:

"What is this?" asks the Lord. "Why are my people enslaved again? Those who rule them shout in exultation. [a] My name is blasphemed all day long.[b] But I will reveal my name to my people, and they will come to know its power. Then at last they will recognize that I am the one who speaks to them."
Isaiah 52: 5-6 (NLT)

CHAPTER TWO

Dare to Dream

> *(Zelophehad, son of Hepher had no sons; he had only daughters, whose names were Mahlah, Noah, Hoglah, Milcah and Tirzah.)*
>
> NUMBERS 26:33 (NIV)

At first glance, this statement may seem boring. On the contrary, it is filled with revelation and insight.

Maybe you grew up in an environment that left you with emotional scars, feelings of shame or secret pain. This kind of childhood trauma can leave us with damaged emotions and relationship dysfunction. I can remember feeling lonely and discarded. I often experienced outbursts of tears. I felt different than my childhood girlfriends. They had fathers in their home who loved and cherished them, while my father was absent. Often, negative words spoken over us as children or even as adults can make us feel unfit, devalued and worthless. A sense of inadequacy plagues our lives and as a result, we resist applying ourselves to a desired end. We forfeit goals and dreams due to a fear of failure. If any of this describes you, then you can take a lesson from the daughters of Zelophehad.

Many of us have been dominated by fear at one time or another in our life. These fears often affect us socially and influence how we interact with others. We fear failure, so we don't try. We fear rejection so we avoid relationships. We fear abandonment so we avoid commitment. We fear criticism and so we overly compensate in an effort to please. We even fear disappointment so we avoid expectation of others or ourselves. Fear will always come knocking on our door but we do not have to open up to it.

Zelophehad Had No Heir

These daughters grew up in an environment that did not accommodate the dreams and visions of most little girls. Their background was not conducive for success. Their family situation was not exactly unwavering and their father did not initially possess the ability to move beyond his own fears to provide them with the secure, stable conditions that little girl's (and most women) best thrive in.

At the time of Zelophehad's death, he had no sons, *"but only daughters."* Therefore, Zelophehad had not produced an heir.

In the eyes of his male counterparts - he, having 'only daughters,' had no successor to receive his inheritance.

As a result, Zelophehad's portion would be passed on to the next qualifying males in the clan upon his death, or thrown back into the pot and dispersed among the tribe.

The fact that a man had no sons, but *"only daughters"* was considered a state or condition of being dishonored or possibly having a deficit of favor, for God had given him no sons.

Not having a son brought a sense of shame and disgrace upon Zelophehad. Many frowned upon this amiable father believing him to be the blame or at fault for not being able to produce a male child. This indicated a sign of weakness in their eyes and a blow to Zelophehad's manhood.

The phrase, *"but only daughters,"* is also an insult to these women, as they did not carry the same status as a man in those days. They were not shown the same degree of dignity, honor or respect. Being a woman automatically signified they were considered lower in rank, position, or standing.

However, like any good father, Zelophehad had a dream for his daughters. He resisted fear and sought to overcome it so that he could provide his daughters with a far better life than he knew. He wanted his daughters to enjoy a future filled with the fruits of his labor. He dreamed of a day when he might enjoy life on the other side of the wilderness with his daughters.

Fear is often learned behavior and characteristically passed down from generation to generation. The names of Zelophehad and his father, Hepher, tell us that fear followed this family.

Never Let Your Family History Dictate Your Destiny

The first step to eradicating repetitive cycles of behavior in your family history is to identify them. It seems Zelophehad's family had experienced significant trouble with fear. We know that his name meant "Shadow of fear". However, His father's name was "Hepher" which meant – pit or ditch.

The 'Shadow of fear' and 'Pit' are closely related.
A pit or ditch can be a frightening place. If one falls into a pit or ditch, he might feel abandoned, discarded or forsaken. If left alone

too long, it might even prove fatal. We do not know exactly what role this pit or ditch played in Hepher's life, but it apparently left a deep emotional scar on him.

If you are walking under a cloud of darkness, Isaiah 9:2 tells us:

> "The people who walk in darkness will see a great light. The light will shine on those living in the land of dark shadows." (NLV)

Scripture promises us that no matter how deep we fall, God's great light will always shine through, leading the way up and out. He is an ever-present help in time of trouble (Ps. 46:1).

God delivered Zelophehad from his shadow of fear. He kept his foot from slipping into the darkness. God did not allow the darkness to invade Zelophehad's mind. His darkness did not keep God from seeing him and did not stop God from loving him right where he was. Zelophehad was in the darkness but the darkness was not allowed to take up residence in him.

You need to know that God sees through your darkness. Nothing is hidden from His eyes concerning you. Scripture assures us that He is the God who sees.

I love 2 Samuel 22:29 which says: "You, Lord, are my lamp; the Lord turns my darkness into light. (NIV)

I can't help but wonder if in addition to Hepher's own personal experience, perhaps the family continued to rehearse the story to him on numerous occasions as he was growing up. Hearing their words only further petrified Hepher. These terrifying promptings alone can instill trepidation in the heart of a child. At any rate, Hepher remained so traumatized – that his experience inspired the name of his son, Zelophehad.

Another word for pit is 'quarry' which means: prey, victim or target.

It is no wonder that *"shadow of fear"* resulted from such a dreadful experience. This was certainly enough to make Hepher feel like a prey, a victim or a target.

This kind of mindset can produce distrust, suspicion, obsession and a victim mentality.

Unintentional Lessons

Through life's journey, we sometime find ourselves following paths of familiarity. We replicate the lives of our ancestors. I am sure Hepher did not intend for his pit experience to influence his son, Zelophehad. Nor did Zelophehad intentionally pass his fear onto his children. However, the story reveals this as the exact outcome.

As a young mother, due to circumstances beyond my control, I became very insecure with a low self-image and low self-esteem. Life's lessons and circumstances left me feeling inadequate. What I did not realize, was that much of my experience was the result of a recurring cycle and learned behavior.

I put on an air of being resilient and independent. Nonetheless, I was simply covering up the deep insecurities within. In so doing, I believe that I unknowingly passed some of these 'insecurities', low self-esteem and fears on to my children. To the contrary, when I invited Christ into my heart and made Him my Lord and Savior, God delivered me.

Along Came a Dreamer

I find it interesting that Zelophehad and his father Hepher, were direct descendants of Joseph. Joseph had a dream and his brothers despised him for it. He was actually thrown into a pit by his jealous brothers and sold into Egypt (Gen. 37:20). He later went to prison. However, he eventually became Pharaoh's Prime Minister and God used his experience to put him into the destiny planned for him all along. Joseph's pit did not destroy him or stop his destiny: God used it to develop and equip him for a far greater purpose than he or his brothers could have imagined. This experience not only put Joseph into the destiny planned for him, but through it, he developed the character required to keep him there.

This information is awe inspiring, as it shows us that no matter how routinely it seems we fall or fail in life - God will cause all things to work together for our good. (Rom.8:28)

Breaking Repetitive Cycles

Perhaps you can identify such a history of events in your own family. Let's say: your grandparents suffered a divorce - then consequently, your mother and father went through a divorce. You swore this would never happen to you. However, you too, without warning, find yourself on the verge of divorce. It is possible that your children will go through a divorce as well unless this vicious cycle is broken. Unfortunately, not every marriage is reconcilable. However, you can recover after such loss. For those seeking to restore a broken marriage, it will take an allegiance to Jesus Christ - disavowing any and all other allegiances, and a complete devotion to your marriage. You and your spouse must make a conscious decision to make Jesus Lord over your lives and over your relationship. As each of you walk out Christ's principles in your own marriage, you will experience a glorious transformation. A self-centered marriage is doomed for destruction, but a Christ centered marriage will not only survive but thrive.

I have seen cycles of alcoholism, drug addiction, multiple incarcerations and other lifestyles and behaviors passed down through generations. Though we call it 'learned behavior', scripture tells us that the curse causeless shall not come (Prov. 26:2). Therefore, we must remove or nullify the cause (reason, source or root) in order to experience freedom.

The root often starts with a broken or wounded heart. We suffered an offense or disappointment that left our heart fertile ground for enemy seeds of deception. We are bombarded with his lies. We build walls to defend our inaccurate perceptions about God and others. We live our lives guarded, on edge and self-justifying.

Our perception of God's word is distorted, and we begin to believe that He no longer loves us. We think that He has abandoned us. This could not be further from the truth. God has equipped and empowered us to break free through the name of Jesus and the authority of His word. The moment we recognize or identify a root (or stronghold) in our lives - all we have to do is repent, forgive anyone involved (including ourselves), and surrender to Christ. He came to bind up the broken hearted and to set the captives free. This is the primary foundational principle for walking out a life of victory over the enemy.

The enemy uses our past to intimidate us and make us feel hopeless, useless and insignificant. This causes us to abandon our hopes and dreams. As a result, we settle for less than God's best for our lives. We develop a false sense of security thinking if we do nothing, we have nothing to lose. We forget the promises of God and start to pursue the thoughts and imaginations of our own wounded heart.

The heart is deceitfully wicked. When our heart is wounded because of pain, rejection, disappointment and abandonment, we typically exude bitterness, anger and retaliation. Consequently, we set ourselves up for more pain as we go through life carrying the proverbial *"chip on our shoulders"*.

God wants to help us break free from the pain of our past. He does not erase the memory completely, but simply removes the pain associated with it. He wants us to learn from our mistakes and see our past failures as springboards to greatness. He will use the unpleasant things of our past to propel us into a destiny that exceeds our utmost dreams or imaginations.

You Are Destined for Greatness

"he[a] predestined us for adoption to sonship[b] through Jesus Christ, in accordance with his pleasure and will—"
Eph. 1:5(NIV)

We are destined for greatness, not failure and defeat. It is the good pleasure of His will that we live our lives as His dear sons and daughters. We've been adopted into the Family of God through Jesus Christ and His shed blood. This blood substantiates, confirms and verifies that we've been born into the family of God.

He freely bestowed his glorious grace upon us. His unmerited (undeserved, unjustified, unwarranted, unearned) favor! This did not occur because we deserved it but simply because He loves us.

The Power of a Name

The name of a child was customarily connected to the family history or to the child's destiny. Therefore, a name was given after much thought. It carried with it a transference of one's identity, purpose, description and/or some specific meaning as with the daughters of Zelophehad.

Before the blessings of God could flow freely upon the lives of Zelophehad and his daughters, it was evident that a change had to take place. Fear and faith cannot coincide with one another. The One will cancel out the other. Fear and Faith cannot be roommates, partners or cohabitate harmoniously.

For the One Living Under the Shadow of Fear, Fear Becomes the Canvas that Every Decision and Every Choice in Life is Painted Upon.

Fear controls every decision. It becomes a filter that every thought, every dream, every desire must pass through before we take action. It debilitates and symptomatically paralyzes us so that our thoughts, dreams and desires are never actually realized. Fear will stop a person from traveling to new places, making commitments, getting married, having children, taking on new opportunities, pursuing a career, purchasing a home and will generally affect every area of life.

Depression is largely associated with the 'shadow of fear'. The enemy uses depression as we keep our focus on ourselves and our circumstances. As a result, we get our mind off the promises of God and thereby refuse to receive His peace. That's why we are told in Ephesians 5:19, to *"speak to ourselves"*. How? In psalms, hymns and spiritual songs, singing and making melody in our hearts.

Let's read what the following verse says concerning fear:

Psalm 56: 3 – 4: "*When I am afraid, I put my trust in you. In God, whose word I praise—in God I trust and am not afraid. What can mere mortals do to me?*" (NIV)

What is this scripture telling us to do when we are afraid?
- Put our trust in God.
- Praise God for His promises.
- Refuse to be afraid of ordinary man (or circumstances).
- Do it by choice! (We may have to do it afraid, but do it anyway).

Turn Opposition into Opportunity

We fear that opposition will destroy us; therefore, we aggressively resist it. We fear that the results of opposing circumstances will negatively affect our possibilities and most likely alter our destiny.

Our dreams and hopes begin to fade. Fear causes many dreams to become buried in the grave of hopelessness and despair. Due to fear, we lose sight of the vision we initially possessed and we cash it in for status quo. However, once we put our trust in the Lord, He will resurrect our dreams and visions as well as reveal the destiny He has for each of us. As we focus on Christ instead of the opposition, fear will lose its power.

Imagination Will Take You to Your Destination

The bible also tells us that without a vision man perish (*to be destroyed violently*). Without a vision (*divine image or visualization for life*), we find ourselves on a path never intended. Fear robs us of the ability to imagine ourselves achieving greatness or visualize ourselves accomplishing lofty exploits. *Imagination is inspiration, inventiveness, dreams, resourcefulness and creativity.* Use your imagination. See yourself walking in your destiny. Find scripture promises to support your dreams and prophesy to yourself, speaking God's life-giving word into your future. When we meditate on His promises, they replace hope for despair. Imagination includes meditation. Meditate means to *'cogitate' - to think deeply about a matter, reflect, or to roll it over in your mind.* The daughters of Zelophehad saw themselves standing before the tribal leaders and the congregation well before they actually stepped into the entrance of the tabernacle. If you are sick, imagine yourself well. If your marriage is in trouble, find scripture promises and speak them over you and your spouse. If you worry over children who are outside of God's will, declare household salvation. Imagine your marriage healed. Envision your children giving their hearts completely to Christ and walking out their days living in freedom and experiencing joy and peace.

Without a Vision, We Lose Hope and Live in Absolute Despair

Remember Joseph, who stepped into his divine destiny as a direct result of opposition. Despite all the things that attempted to put off his destiny, he prevailed. He emerged triumphant.

As you will recall, we talked about how Joseph survived being thrown into the pit, sold into slavery and then into prison, but eventually became governor to Pharaoh and ended up in the palace as the 'number two' man over the Kingdom. What we also need to realize is that his position provided him the opportunity to give food to his brothers during a famine. He saw the father whom he thought he'd never see again and the breach between him and his brothers were utterly reconciled. In addition to all this, the whole nation and surrounding people were blessed with provisions during the famine.

His personal victory became a victory for many. What God makes happen for us usually benefits others as well. God's plan is bigger and far spread than we can imagine.

It is not opposition that defeats us - it is our response to opposition. It is not actually fear that paralyzes us. It is our perception regarding a thing or situation that causes us to become overwhelmed. What we believe about our lives influences what we imagine for our lives and what we imagine will eventually become our reality. The scripture tells us that as a man devises (plans, invents, schemes or conceives), in his heart, so is he (Prov. 23:7).

Reflections

Dare to Dream
Chapter Two

1). Many of us have been dominated by fear at one time or another in our life. We fear failure, rejection, abandonment, commitment, criticism and disappointment.

> *If any of these applies to you, where are you now in terms of fears influence and effects on your life? What have you done or are you doing to break their control?*

2). Never let your family history dictate your destiny. The first step to eradicating repetitive cycles of behavior in your family history is to identify them.

> *Are there family traits and characteristics that seem to plague you or your family? What are they?*

3). Though we find it hard to believe, opposition has the ability to thrust us into the plans and purposes that God intended for us from the beginning. Think about and/or discuss the following scripture and how it may apply to you:

> *2 Corinthians 4:17-18: "For our light and momentary troubles are achieving for us an eternal glory that far outweighs them all. So, we fix our eyes not on what is seen, but on what is unseen, since what is seen is temporary, but what is unseen is eternal." (NIV)*

Scriptural Inheritance Affirmation:

"Why would you ever complain...saying, "God has lost track of me. He doesn't care what happens to me"? Don't you know anything? Haven't you been listening? God doesn't come and go. God lasts. He's Creator of all you can see or imagine. He doesn't get tired out, doesn't pause to catch his breath. And he knows everything, inside and out. He energizes those who get tired, gives fresh strength to dropouts..." Isaiah 40: 27-29 (MSG)

CHAPTER THREE

"The Apple of the Eye"

The Hebrew word for daughter is "Beth". The actual definition is; 'apple of the eye, the most dearly loved person, and one who is as precious as sight itself.'

Though Zelophehad had no sons, his daughters were the apple of his eye. He treasured his daughters and nothing indicates that he loved them any less. Not only were they the apple of their father's eye, but through them God would provide a legacy beyond anything Zelophehad could conceive. His daughters would be world changers and history makers. They would one day turn their culture upside down.

The Big Reveal: Five Names That Tell a Profound Story

Now let me introduce you to these phenomenal women:

> "...The names of Zelophehad's daughters were Mahlah, Noah, Hoglah, Milcah and Tirzah. Num. 26:33 (NLV)

Fear had such a stronghold in Zelophehad's life that it induced the names of his first two daughters. Let's take a look at their names and see what they mean.

This dramatic story begins to open up with the birth of the first daughter.

Allow me to introduce you to Mahlah:

"Mahlah" means – "Disease"

Disease is fear's consequence on our physical body:

It creates an environment conducive for sickness to develop and spread like a festering sore. Science tells us that fear weakens our immune system leaving the body susceptible to poor health.

Proverbs 14:30 backs up this belief saying: *"A sound mind makes for a robust body, but runaway emotions corrode the bones... MSG"*

Fear causes the bones (the skeletal frame), to disintegrate according to this scripture. This means, the bones oxidize, degenerate or wear away. These bones then are easily fractured or broken.

Worry is A Direct Result of Fear

We don't know just how or when this disease developed, but we know that it had to be early on in order for Zelophehad to name her, 'Mahlah' or 'Disease'.

According to multiple sources, many stomach disorders, skin diseases and severe headaches/migraines can time and again be traced back to fear.

Let me introduce you to the second daughter:
'Noah'.
Her name means – 'Trembling'

Trembling is fears consequence on the mind and emotions.

Based on my own experience with fear, it not only causes physical harm to the body, but also mental and emotional distress. It produces hopelessness, oppression and even suicidal tendencies. Fear causes insomnia, anxiety and trembling.

These feelings of revulsion and dreadfulness cause the body to respond in *"trembling"*. Have you ever been so afraid that you froze in panic? You wanted to run but you couldn't move. Fear can paralyze you and cause your whole body to quiver as if you were having convulsions.

Then a third daughter, Hoglah was born:

Here we sense something new and exciting happening. Her name means "Caller" which indicates that Zelophehad begin to "Call" out: By this time, it appears that a shift took place in the life of Zelophehad. It is apparent that Zelophehad had a transformation of heart. He grew increasingly weary of fear controlling and dominating his life. It had already influenced Mahlah and Noah so he resolved to put an end to it. As a result, he set out to take action that would destroy fear forever.

This is a turning point for Zelophehad. No matter what we go through in life, if we hold on to God's unchanging hand, there will always be a turning point. The very thing that the enemy meant to destroy us can be the very thing that drives us to a place of calling out to God in desperation.

Zelophehad began to call out to God in the midst of his circumstance. We're not referring to a casual call; he called out loud, hard, fervently, persistently and with great determination. He became desperate for a breakthrough.

Hoglah further denotes one who is a 'chatterer'.

This indicates repetition. One who calls repeatedly.

I believe he didn't just have a little talk with Jesus, but rather 'prayed fervently', as one who labored strenuously in prayer (Col.4:12). This is a teeth-clinching, fist-pounding, brow-sweating, floor pacing prayer. Some of you know what I'm talking about. It's often described as 'bearing down hard' in prayer. This prayer was tenacious and fitful.

Agreeably, we know God hears our prayers and it doesn't require everything described here to get a prayer through.

However, nothing will drive a parent to their knees like seeing their children suffering under the attack of the enemy.

All tolerance goes out the door when we see our children hurting or suffering. Unfortunately, we typically give up just before the birthing of our miracle. Just when the labor gets intense, we grow faint. This is the time not to faint but rather, to push harder. We must be willing to PRESS through prayerfully – *"Pray Relentlessly, Earnestly, Steadfastly and Single-mindedly."*

Isaiah 32:9 extends such a prayer call, telling the *women who are unreasonably content, excessively relaxed or extensively gratified to rise up.*

In verse 12, He tells them to "beat their breasts", which is a term used in some cultures referring to passionate prayer. This statement is referring to unrelenting and hammering prayer. It required the banishing of their lethargy and complacency, in preparation to resist the pronouncement of evil against them or for whom they must pray.

He continues to tell them in verse 15, to pray until *"the Spirit is poured from on high."* Then, don't stop there, but keep on praying *"until the desert becomes a fertile field and until the fertile field becomes a forest."* (NIV)

In other words, don't stop short - pray until you get the full manifestation of your expectation.

God Puts the Final Touch on the Tapestry of Our Lives

The tapestry of their lives appeared to be finally coming together exhibiting all the beauty and spender of a glorious portrait painted by the grace of God. The struggle they endured and the prayers Zelophehad prayed culminated together and now God was applying the final touch *"on them'* and *"to them"*.

As a result of calling out to God, Zelophehad began to hear God responding to his cry.

Here, the fourth daughter takes center stage. Allow me to introduce you to *"Milcah"*.

Her name means *"Counsel"*.

When Zelophehad cried out to the Lord, God gave him counsel.

The definition for Counsel is – Deliberate purpose, plan, or intent. It is not just mere advice, opinion, ideas, or suggestions.

That's what God will do for you too when you cry out to Him. He has a deliberate, purposeful and intentional plan concerning you. That thing you are going through is designed to turn in your favor.

Suddenly Zelophehad begins to understand that despite the opposition he faced; God had a plan for him and for his daughters.

Last but not least, the fifth daughter is born:

Allow me to present Zelophehad's youngest daughter. She is the one who finalizes this fascinating story in joyful and harmonious fashion. Like the crescendo of a glorious melodious concert, she steps up to the podium of life, positions herself in this line of phenomenal births and leaves us with an experience that is transforming and exceedingly joyous.

Her name is Tirzah which means Delight.

Delight means happiness, pleasure, joy, enchantment, glee, gladness, amusement.

God Promises to Turn Our Mourning into Dancing

When we call out to Him, He is there to rescue us from all our anxieties and to deliver us from all our fears. For those who seek His counsel, He will give wisdom, direction and knowledge - and for those who have lost their joy, He will enrich their lives with renewed hope, fulfillment and delight in Him again.

Gods *"Counsel" produced "Delight"*. Finally, it seems the ordeal was over and the calamity broken from the lives of Zelophehad and his daughters, but it is far from the end of this story.

It is no coincidence that each daughter's name ends with *"Ah"*

"Ah" represents the names of Jehovah God such as Jehovah JIRA (The Lord our Provider), Jehovah RAPHA (The Lord our healer), Jehovah SHALOM (The Lord our peace), Jehovah 'EZER (The Lord Our Help), Jehovah SHAMMAH (The Ever Present One), Jehovah ROHI (The Lord our Shepherd) Jehovah GÂ 'AL (THE LORD THY REDEEMER KINSMAN and Jehovah TSIDKENU (The Lord our Righteousness), just to name a few. Each one indicates His provision. (Bible Names of God.com and Wikipedia.com)

Though each name appeared to tell a riveting story - with each name, Zelophehad proclaimed God to be the fullness of his expectation. If you are going through a dark place and need God to show up on your behalf, know that He is willing to rescue you. His names indicate His very nature, character and attributes. By His mighty power, He will thrust you forward, upward and onward. Like Zelophehad, endeavor to invoke His name in the midst of your opposition and calamity by declaring who He is and decreeing His promises.

Finally, after many years of living under the Shadow of Fear - like the breaking forth of the radiant sun after a turbulent day, Zelophehad was set free!

Zelophehad (Shadow of fear) produced Disease and Trembling, but when he Called out to God, God gave him Counsel and Counsel produced Delight.

Live a Life of No Limits

Know that your life is not limited by the inabilities to meet the unrealistic demands and expectations of others or the inadequate resources surrounding you. God has fully equipped you for the course He set before you and He has enabled you by His grace, (Devine enablement and empowerment), to accomplish all that He has for your life. It is by His grace that we are saved. His grace reached down to a people not worthy of His kindness, yet He pardoned us from our sin by the precious blood of His own Son, Jesus Christ. This same grace continues to work in us today as His followers. He is at work in you both to give you the 'will' to fulfill his plan and the 'ability' to carry it out to completion.

Ezekiel 12:25 tells us *"Because I am the Lord, I'll speak and the message that I communicate will be accomplished without delay…"* (ISV)

The fulfillment of your dreams, passions, plans, aspiration or destiny may seem to be delayed but that does not mean they are denied.

The bible tells us that we are God's workmanship:

"For we are his workmanship, created in Christ Jesus for good works, which God prepared beforehand, that we should walk in them." (Eph. 2:10) ESV

This indicates a master-piece, work of art or a skillfully (capably, proficiently), grafted image.

I recently woke up one morning with these words of blessing & affirmation in my ear:

> *"You have great purpose, extreme potential, are highly valued and significant. No one can do what you do, be who you are designed to be or accomplish what you are called to accomplish. There is only one you in all the earth. Your thumb print is proof that you are unique. Know that when you were created, excellence was imparted to you - success was designed for you, hope was established in you and love was bestowed upon you. You are a joy to the heart of others and celebrated by all who truly know and love you. You are fully capable, totally equipped and well able to fulfill the dreams and aspirations that I have put in your heart. Your presence brings comfort, peace and hope. Your life is a gift. Live it fully, embrace it joyfully and share it generously"*

As God spoke these words to me, they felt like a liquid healing balm as they flowed deep down inside of my being. They were soothing and comforting to parts of my inner self that no man could ever touch. I pray that you will receive this affirmation today and know that you too are precious! You are incredible! In the eyes of your heavenly father, there is no one like you.

God uses ordinary people to do extraordinary things

God uses the least likely individuals in a family to rise up and make a positive difference. He uses regular, ordinary people like you and me to do unusual or unconventional things.

God takes the inadequate individual and makes them entirely adequate to perform beyond their capacity.

Paul also tells us in 2 Corinthians 3: 5-6: *"Not that we are competent (capable, knowledgeable, experienced, proficient or skilled), of ourselves to claim anything as coming from us; our competence (ability, expertise, know-how, qualifications), is from God, who has made us competent to be ministers…". We were not competent, sufficient, capable or adequate in ourselves, God "made" us adequate as his servants.* (NRSV)

We cannot accomplish God's plan for our lives by trusting in our own strength or in our own intellect. We do not possess the skill to do so within our own power. Like the daughters of Zelophehad, God uses the least likely individuals to accomplish great feats. He uses ordinary people to do extraordinary exploits and common folk to accomplish uncommon acts of victory.

You may have been voted the least likely to succeed in life in your high school yearbook, but He will use the least likely individual to accomplish enormous outcomes. He set His seal of approval upon us before we were created within our mother's womb. Therefore, we need not seek approval, validation or confirmation from any man.

Our heavenly Father genuinely loves us. We can't run fast enough or far enough to out run God's love. His love will out run the mightiest in strength and power, go further than the east is from the west and out last time and eternity.

God's Work on Display

"Zelophehad had no sons, but only daughters." While some thought this was an indication that he was unable to produce an heir or that God

somehow was not pleased with him - on the contrary, God allowed Zelophehad's plight so that His works could be put on display.

It was not a coincidence that Zelophehad had only daughters.

God takes the things we consider 'a quandary, challenge, trouble' or even what seems useless, inadequate or an absolute mess and He turns it around for the Master's use.

Like the potter's clay, though it was marred (blemished, stained, flawed or disfigured), He didn't dispose of it. Instead, He took that same lump of clay and molded and reshaped it into something exquisitely beautiful. (Jeremiah 18: 1- 4)

The daughters of Zelophehad were flawed because of their father's fear. Their future seemed marred by the damage it caused. They bore the stain of fears imperfections, blemished by its stigmas and were emotionally disfigured.

Marred clay is considered damaged goods and of no use, but in the eyes of the Master it appears extraordinary, notable, astonishing, outstanding and amazing. Only God can make something extraordinary out of that which man calls common, damaged or ordinary.

Man may consider an individual to be insignificant, irrelevant and unimportant - but God highly values His creation. We were made in His own image and likeness. He will put Himself on display in our lives if we will trust Him.

The Power of Relationships

The daughters of Zelophehad maintained a deep relationship with each other throughout their lives. We know that sisters characteristically experience disagreements and do not always see eye to eye. However, it seems that they were able to work through any sibling difficulties and overcome potential hurdles. It is not always obvious who God will use to help us reach our destiny. Therefore, it is wise to protect the relationships we have and not make rash decisions to sever them.

Reflections

"The Apple of the Eye"
Chapter Three

1). The Hebrew word for daughter is "Beth". The actual definition is; "apple of the eye, and one who is as precious as sight itself."

> Can you think of a scripture or an experience that made you realize that you are so cherished by God?

2). The names of Zelophehad's daughters tell an amazing story and reveal various aspects of who they are in terms of their nature and characteristics.

> What does your life story tell about you based on your name, your nature, personality, attributes and/or characteristics? What are your greatest qualities?

3). God takes the inadequate individual and makes them completely adequate to perform beyond their capacity. Review and discuss/think about the following scripture.

> 2 Corinthians 3: 5-6, Paul also tells us: "Not that we are competent (capable, knowledgeable, experienced, proficient or skilled), of ourselves…our competence (ability, expertise, qualifications), is from God…"

4). Now think about or discuss what this means to you.

Marred clay is viewed as 'damaged goods.' God sees you as extraordinary, notable, astonishing, outstanding and amazing.

How has your relationship with Christ changed how you see yourself now?

Scriptural Inheritance Affirmation:

"I am God, the only God you've had or ever will have—incomparable, irreplaceable—from the very beginning telling you what the ending will be. All along letting you inon what is going to happen, assuring you, "I'm in this for the long haul, I'll do exactly what I set out to do," Isaiah 46:9-11 (MSG)

CHAPTER FOUR

Causing to Forget

Zelophehad was a member of the Tribe of '*Manasseh*'. Manasseh means; 'causing to forget'.

The enemy tries to harass, torment and intimidate us. He wants to cause us to forget God by focusing on our past fears, future concerns and/or our present circumstances more than the promises of God.

Though they struggled, the Tribe of Manasseh refused to forget about God and the mighty things He had done for them. We've all been in a pit one time or another. Whenever we are in a pit, we must practice rehearsing the things God has already done for us. The more we rehearse the ways in which God has shown up for us in the past – the more we will be encouraged to wait on Him in present difficulties.

If a father loses his footing in life due to the snares, traps and pit-falls the enemy sets before him - his children are customarily negatively influenced as well. However, when that father regains his footing like Zelophehad, he repositions himself. In doing so, he shows his children how to get back up after a fall and positions his family for generational blessings. We too can always turn our troubles into triumphs by bringing to mind and recollecting the exploits of our God.

What should we remember when we are in the pit you may ask?

- Cry out to God
- Seek His counsel (deliberate purpose, plan and intent)
- Listen for His response
- Remember His past goodness and faithfulness
- Seek His presence
- Commit yourself to Him and Trust Him
- Remember His promises
- Delight in Him through times of Worship

Combined Strengths

The daughters of Zelophehad combined their strengths in order to accomplish their goal.

Each one contributed the needed character, personality and attribute to help the other and support their efforts. They had one heart, one mind and one goal.

The world gives women a bad reputation by saying that women can't work together. The daughters of Zelophehad prove that women can work in partnership together and accomplish great achievements.

Normally the older siblings pave the way for the younger, but God has a way of going against what we consider normal in order to accomplish exceptional results. He takes the unexpected, least qualified person and causes him/her to flourish, thrive and go all the way to the top. Of course, it goes without saying, that if Disease and Tremble had not experienced physical disparity resulting from their father's fear - Zelophehad may have never become tenacious enough to defeat his enemy.

These two daughters were the fuel that ignited the fire in Zelophehad for change. As a result, they too were delivered and made whole, so that they could reclaim their destiny.

It was most likely the sister, Caller, who summoned the sisters together to discuss the possibilities of requesting their father's inheritance. She was the vocal one. She was accustomed to having her voice heard when she spoke.

I see the other sister, Counsel, as the one who probably provided direction and advice to the group. She was the advocate they needed to support and encourage each one to stay on track.

The last sister, Delight, was the one who most likely kept everything on a happy note and made certain they maintained their focus on the end result. She reminded them that the outcome would far exceed any physical, emotional or cultural peril they would face.

However, Disease and Tremble were not without their contribution. Once they got on board with the idea, they encouraged the sisters to go all the way. They understood that nothing came without a price.

Treasure the Gift That You Are

The three younger daughters of Zelophehad could have easily discounted the value of the first two sisters because they were most affected by their father's fear. Their initial impact was far more devastating than that of the younger girls. However, they chose to recognize each sister's significance and usefulness to their cause. They realized that their personal experience did not omit their worth or reduce their capabilities

> *1 Peter 4: 10-11 "As each has received a gift, use it to serve one another, as good stewards of God's varied grace... as one who serves by the strength that God supplies—in order that in everything God may be glorified through*

Jesus Christ. To him belong glory and dominion forever and ever. Amen."(ESV)

Breaking New Ground

The Lord told Moses and Eleazar to take a census of Israel from ages 20 and older. The census bought them all together in one place for this specific occasion.

A procession of young men stepped forward as the list of several individual families was called.

The procession came to a screeching halt as we approach verse 1, (Numbers 27). Here, we are unexpectedly introduced to the daughters of Zelophehad when they shockingly appeared in the doorway of the Tabernacle. There must have been a stirring in the crowd as the men whispered to each other in amazement and wondered what just happened. Some probably glared at the women in astonishment and disapproval.

It was recorded in the chronicles with a note of disbelief and bewilderment as the writer recalled that day when the daughters of Zelophehad came before Moses, all the tribal leaders and the congregation to present their petition. It was as if to say - the census was going well up to this point, then, out from nowhere, Zelophehad's daughters suddenly appeared. Everything seemed to shift for a moment. No one could have predicted such a seemingly appalling thing would have transpired right in the middle of a highly structured and customary event.

The daughters of Zelophehad were breaking new ground and they were upsetting the metaphorical apple cart in the eyes of the leaders and congregation. It was destined that their father would have no sons - only daughters.

We Must Have a 'No Turning Back Mentality'

Many of us desire to grow stronger in our walk with the Lord, but aren't willing to put aside the distractions and other diversions - such as entertainment or hobbies in order to spend the necessary time in the word of God or in prayer to accomplish the goal. We want a better marriage but take on a "what's in it for me" attitude, rather than seeking how we may serve our spouse according to the principles laid out for us in God's word. We desire financial success, but want to spend money needlessly on things that are "wants" instead of "needs". I have been guilty of all of these things until I realized that repeating the same behavior will only give me the same results and if I wanted change, then I had to be willing to make some changes in my life. Once initiated, it required a no turning back mentality.

One Day Can Make All the Difference

The daughters of Zelophehad had waited a very long time for this day. Now that it was finally here, they knew that it would be a day like no other. Perhaps you've had to wait for something for a long time. Waiting is never easy but it is necessary. It takes patience, expectation and commitment. We wait in theater lines, concert halls, airports, medical offices, restaurants and other establishments all because we are hopeful that eventually we will get whatever it is we are waiting for. During the wait, we have to resist frustration, irritation, negative self-talk and opposing voices as well as the temptation to simply turn and walk away.

After years of the same protocol, all of a sudden, there they stood. While we face arduous times, these women suffered a very different standard of living and traditional concepts than we know and experience today.

This was a true test of their freedom from fear. These daughters were on a mission and they were about to change history.

We repeatedly say, 'one day' I will do this, or I will do that, only to never have it come to pass because we procrastinate or allow things to get in our way.

We frequently come before God asking for His intervention in our complex lives. We pray and seek God sometime for days, weeks, months or even years. We read the word of God hoping for a solution. Then all of a sudden - when we least expect it, God breaks forth on our behalf.

The daughters of Zelophehad relished in the fact that this day was the answer to their long-awaited prayers. They yearned for it ever since their father's death. They imagined what it would be like when this day finally arrived.

Don't Give Up Prematurely

Several of us are standing at the threshold of our destiny, but give up prematurely.

There are those who have asked, but have grown weary of waiting when the answer was delayed. Though seemingly deferred, it will come in God's time.

The daughters of Zelophehad had no idea that they were literally standing at the threshold of their destiny. They were right on the verge of their breakthrough. As they stood at the doorsill of the tabernacle, they were on the brink of a miracle. You may be standing at the threshold of your healing, deliverance, financial breakthrough, birthing of a ministry or achieving household salvation. Someone may be right at the unveiling of restoration in your marriage or reconciliation in a valued relationship. The darkest hour is just before day. Hang in there. Don't give up prematurely.

Releasing Our Unlocked Potential

Many of us have locked potential inside us just waiting to be revealed. The daughters of Zelophehad had an overwhelming desire to pursue their father's inheritance. This intensity unlocked the potential in each of these five sisters.

Great opportunities often come out of great adversities. However, you don't have to wait until an adversity to unlock your potential. God will ignite a passion within you through prayer, worship and the reading of His word. Fellowship with other strong believers, or consider finding an accountability partner. Seek a mentor who is actively walking in the gifts and talents not yet fully developed within you.

Discover your passion. What excites you? Passion is a driving force that compels you to act, as a result of the deep desire, fervor or appetite for change.

Allow God to awaken the unlocked potential He deposited in you. Fan the flame within you by taking a leap of faith. Take action! Start practicing your gift or endowment. Begin writing those songs, organizing those sermons, practicing the art of liturgical dance, formulating poems or preparing in advance by appropriating your talents before the door opens. Don't wait until opportunity knocks. Practice the presence of God. The emergence of your greatest potential may be birthed as a result of the very opposition you are currently facing.

Step out with confidence in order to achieve that which is possible - though not yet actual.

The lessons you learn through life's adversities will help equip you so that you will nurture the excellence and characteristics needed to sustain you. Once you reach your goal - you will have staying power.

Destiny may be accomplished during stages or phases in our lives. They are not all simultaneous or concurrent one with another. There are often interludes, intermissions or recesses when we feel like we are not useful at all. These are merely pauses while God reconstructs or recalculates our pathway.

I left my hometown to relocate forty years ago; it was initially fear that drove me to make the decision to move. God later set me free, but not before using fear to push me into a destiny experience. Within six months - I had an apartment, a job and quite unexpectedly met my husband.

When it comes to realizing destiny, we find ourselves becoming familiar with doing the one thing or assuming that one thing is our destiny. I have learned that there are appointed times and seasons of destiny in our lives. Ultimately, it's all about serving the Kingdom of God and the Body of Christ.

We All Have Untapped Potential

Untapped potential lies within each of us. However, it remains dormant because of inhibitions resulting from the pain and suffering of life. We don't realize our potential because opposition has left us feeling insecure and with a downcast self-image. In the Book of John, chapter four, we find another fitting and enthralling story about the Samaritan woman at the water well who had five husbands and was living with the sixth man. Jesus was there and weary from his journey, sat down by this well. This was a woman who felt worthless, inadequate and unfit.

This story goes on to tell us that it was noon when the Samaritan woman came to draw water - Jesus asks her for a drink. The Samaritan woman asks Jesus how it is that he, being a Jew, would ask her for a drink. Jesus told her that if she knew the gift of God and who it was doing the asking, she would have asked Him for a drink and He would have given her living water. This intrigued the woman and she ask how He could give her this water since He had nothing to draw with and the well is very deep. Jesus explained to her that everyone who drinks from this well will be thirsty again, but those who drink the water that He offered, would never thirst again. She doesn't fully understand but senses that this is what she had been longing for all of her life. Jesus knew that this woman's thirst was deeper than quenching her physical parchedness. She then left her empty water pots behind and went back and evangelized the whole town. Her untapped potential was released when she met Jesus.

As we embrace our relationship with Christ, our untapped potential is unleashed.

God wants to heal us everywhere we hurt

As we see how the daughters of Zelophehad grew and developed into strong, capable women despite their challenging beginning, we are inspired to discover our own capability as men and women who cry out to God and seek to know Him intimately.

This story of Zelophehad and his daughters gives us hope as we see how God can supersede fear, man's negative influence, and opposing circumstance in our lives as He transforms us into the men and women, He called us to be.

Forgiving Our Past

In order for us to become totally healed from the pain of past hurts and disappointments, we must forgive our past. Forgive ourselves for personal failures and forgive those who have hurt us. Forgive the injustices, prejudice behaviors and all other forms of inflicted pain.

Forgiving our past includes not only the hurtful things of the past but forsaking those good things, those presumed happier times or involvements that cause us to long for prior relationships, prior possessions and previous experiences.

We cannot move forward when our heart is still connected to the past.

In order to release our potential, we must first alter our thinking and our attitudes. Our perception must change. No longer view your life through a mirror looking rearward. You are called to move forward and can only do so by deserting the remorseful things behind you. Abandon reminiscences of your past. Turn a blind eye to mental diaries and discard emotional recollections so that you can rewrite a more fitting story like the daughters of Zelophehad. No matter how the previous chapter of your story is read, you get to determine how your story ends.

Reflections

"Causing to Forget"
Chapter Four

1). The Tribe of Manasseh faltered in their faith but refused to forget God in their distress.

> *Why is it important to remember God and what are some of the things we should remember about Him?*

2). The daughters of Zelophehad were breaking new ground and making a difference.

> *In what way do you desire to make a difference in the lives of others?*

3). We cannot move forward because our heart is still connected to the past.

> *Are you connected to your past because of someone or something you are holding on to?*

4). The daughters of Zelophehad combined their strengths to accomplish their goal.

> *Which of the daughters of Zelophehad do you most identify with and why?*

5). The daughters of Zelophehad possessed hidden potential that was buried under fear until Zelophehad cried out to God.

What unlocked potential have you seen unleashed resulting from embracing Christ more deeply?

Scriptural Inheritance Affirmation:

"They will not work in vain, and their children will not be doomed to misfortune. For they are people blessed by the Lord, and their children, too, will be blessed." Isaiah 65:23 (TLB)

CHAPTER FIVE

Our Beginning Does Not Determine Our End

Some of us can look back at our beginning in life and wonder how we made it this far. I've seen children who grew up in homes where drugs were prevalent and abuse rampant, yet they went on to defeat the odds and break free from the vicious course set before them. Some finished college and became highly productive despite their beginning. I've seen young teenage girls, including myself, become mothers. Some often drop out of school and struggle to raise their child - but many go on to be great mothers, go back to school and accomplish extraordinary success.

Other times, it appears as if we are experiencing the 'beginning of the end'. Our lives can change in an instant. All it takes is one thought, one decision and our lives can turn from one outcome to another. However, God's word tells us that He knows our end before our beginning.

All hope is never lost in such cases. Just as quickly as things appear to go downhill, they can turn again in your favor.

The first two of Zelophehad's daughters started in a seemingly downhill situation. Sickness was beginning to infiltrate their bodies.

I once thought my life was doomed for disaster. I made bad choices that could have left me mentally and emotionally devastated. I had to fight the spirit of rejection, abandonment, guilt and shame until I cried out to God. His indescribable love and acceptance transformed my life. The voids I tried to fill in an attempt to find love and acceptance in bad relationships were happily filled in my relationship with Christ.

Too often, we put our trust in man to appease us. We look to worldly relationships to give us the esteem and value we long for. When that which we have trusted in, relied on and depended upon fails us - it is then when we realize that our trust has been misdirected.

This reminds me of another amazing story in the Bible. In the Book of Ruth, chapter one, we read the story of Naomi. Her husband (Elimelek) died. His name meant *"My King"*. *When Elimelek died, Naomi lost her "King"*. She lost her ruler, manager, director and guide. God alone wants to be all those things to us. Our trust must be in God alone. When she later lost her two sons, whose names meant 'Sickly" and 'Pining Away", the loss was more than she could bear. Overcome by grief, Naomi lost her joy and her song. Her hope was gone. If our joy and our song are predicated in something or someone other than God, we will be severely disappointed when opposition comes. However, when we make Christ our Joy and our Song, we will stand strong against all conflict because He has become our Praise. The bible declares that the Joy of the Lord is our strength! If we lose our Joy, we lose our strength and therefore lose our resistance against the enemy.

You need to know that, because of the power of the greater one inside you, you are stronger than you think you are!

Don't allow opposition to cause you to lose your Joy and your Song.

When Naomi's two sons died, she had nothing to offer her daughters-in-law and felt the need to send them away.

She even changed her name from Naomi, which means 'Joyful' to Mara which means 'Bitter' because she felt that God had allowed her to suffer more than she was able to bear. It seemed even He had left her. Naomi did something many of us do when we are discouraged. She practiced negative self-talk. She didn't realize that negative self-talk only weighs you down further. She didn't realize that in doing so, she was getting in agreement with the enemy. When she changed her name, she was agreeing with her pain and blocking potential forthcoming blessings.

Naomi lost her King, her Joy and her Song, but her two daughters in law - Ruth and Orpha, loved her and wanted to stay with her. Naomi insisted that they each return to their respective families.

Sometimes it seems that the thing we lost is so great, that what remains is diminished. We lose all perspective. Grieving that which is lost overshadows that which is left and we miss out on the joy of what remains.

Interestingly, Ruth's name means (Female Companion), and Orpha means (Turning of the neck). Orpha did as her name proclaims and turned back. She decided to return home to her family and to what was familiar to her - while Ruth proved to be a female friend and companion and stayed with Naomi. Ruth chose to go wherever Naomi went and to lodge wherever Naomi lodged. She declared that Naomi's people would be her people and that Naomi's God would be her God. Little did she know that her selfless determination would thrust her into a glorious life far beyond anything she could have ever foreseen.

God sends Help in Times of Trouble

When Naomi was preoccupied with her pain, God gave her a female companion who would lift her up. Ruth adjoined herself to Naomi in covenant.

Naomi and Ruth left Moab (Land of Seed), to return to Bethlehem (House of Bread). Remember; Naomi and her family initially left Bethlehem to go to Moab because there was a great famine. Now the surviving mother-in-law and daughter-in-law are returning to Bethlehem.

Like many of us, Naomi's family had been living in the *"House of Bread" - but when things looked bleak, they moved to the land of "Seed". Even in that situation, God had a plan. 'Seed' was produced while in Moab, as the beautiful relationship between Naomi and Ruth developed - but now it was time for them to return to the 'House of Bread'. They had no way of knowing that in returning to the 'House of Bread", (where famine once overflowed), they would receive restoration and abundance of joy.*

Isn't that similar to what we do today? Commonly, when we are experiencing a drought in our lives - whether it is finances, health, relationship, etc., we go after strange seed instead of watering the seed and cultivating the soil we already have. It seems God is no longer performing, so we set out to make or create our own success. While leaving is sometime necessary, we must do so prayerfully. Otherwise, we may be acting impulsively or presumptuously.

Only in finding and remaining in the will of God can we acquire true joy and enrichment in our lives. We will bloom when we are planted in the soil that God has purposed for us.

God Holds Us Up and Keeps Our Foot from Slipping

We rarely realize the plan of God for our lives in advance. We need to be content with today and not worry about our future. God promises that if we acknowledge Him in all our ways, He will direct our paths. It may literally be one step at a time.

You may feel like your life, health, finances, marriage, family, career, ministry and such are 'sickly and pining away'. Be still and know that God is able to restore even that which seems dead. He is the Resurrection and the Life!

God will lead us into our destiny

It does not always come natural for us to discern the voice of God in a matter. It's not something that happens instinctively. Our own heart can mislead us and our emotions can demand a particular outcome. The influence of others can cause confusion. At any rate, I want to encourage you to seek the Lord regarding your choices. Confer with God before making reckless decisions. I know many who didn't always do this, including myself - only to regret it. Sensing God's voice becomes clearer as we spend time with Him and practice His presence on a regular basis.

I am happy to say however, that even when I missed God, He lovingly redirected my steps and ultimately brought me onto a path of blessing. It is helpful to submit to your church leaders or have someone to whom you are accountable. *"Plans fail for lack of counsel, but with many advisers they succeed."* Proverbs 15:22 NIV

It was He who held me up and kept my foot from slipping. When I would have taken another path God gently pushed me into an alternate direction. It is God who sustains our coming in and our going out. He secures our footage so that we do not slip or veer into a direction that will take us completely off His plan. Even when we seemingly change course, He uses it like Naomi's family escapade to Moab. We may take what seems like a wrong direction in the natural only to realize it was necessary to the ultimate plan of God.

Why did Ruth follow Naomi?

When the 'seed' of hope had diminished, both women returned to *"the house of bread"*. Ruth gleamed from the field of Boaz, a wealthy kinsmen redeemer of the husband of Naomi to provide food for them. Boaz means 'Strength' (Power, influence, muscle, vigor, intensity, and know how). Boaz possessed everything Ruth needed. God knows how to give you what you need, when you need it!

Boaz saw her, fell in love with her and after seeking her release from the first qualifying kinsmen redeemer, he married her. Together they had a son named Obed, whose name means; servant of God, worshipper. Ruth became ancestress of Jesus Christ. Her son, Obed was the father of Jesse (whose name means 'Jehovah exists'), and Jesse was the father of King David (Beloved one). Even though Naomi's family left Bethlehem to live in a foreign country, and even though their family suffered great loss, God had a plan to bless Naomi. He controlled their destiny - and no amount of loss, bitterness, pain or anything else could stop it from being fulfilled. We can see according to the names of each one listed here that God continued to be glorified throughout generations to come in Naomi's family.

Like the melodic rhythms of a heartbeat, each experience leads us to the next until we reach an obvious destination for our life. Destiny required Ruth to follow Naomi. Living out our destiny is not about one major event or occasion. Some experiences will be more obvious than others, but in following the paths before us as controlled by the

Spirit of God and allowing Him to use our lives at each stage - He will fulfill His plan and purpose through us. In hind sight, we will eventually see the bigger picture and recognize that we've ultimately stepped over various thresholds of destiny.

God's Woman

It's amazing how one verse of scripture can narrate a whole story. By merely examining each name of the Zelophehad family, we discovered a hidden family history and subsequent destiny that is mind boggling.

The daughters of Zelophehad did not allow their circumstances to dictate their character or nature. They were women fashioned by God.

In those days, a woman's testimony would not hold up in a court of law unless corroborated by a man. Otherwise, it would take the testimony of 100 women to equal the testimony of one man.

These remarks are meant only to help women recognize that despite how culture and others may view them, God does not see them as the world does. He sees us as an exquisite treasure, valuable beyond cost, more precious than gold and worthy of celebration.

In Christ's day, we see that He included women. The Jewish Talmud or Mishnah, had different kinds of laws against women. The Talmud is the body of Jewish and Civil laws which some valued higher than the Bible. However, there were obvious women in the genealogy of Jesus Christ, such as Mary, Rahab and Ruth.

Jesus allowed a woman to touch Him, although she was considered unclean, He ate with unsavory women and He met privately with the woman at the well to converse with her about the *"living"* water.

Jesus taught men and women alike. As noted, a woman was obviously present at His birth. Again women were at the cross and at the tomb. Women were involved in these three major milestones of Jesus' life.

We are told that women are frequently rejected and abused. According to Domestic Violence Statistics online report; *"...every 9 seconds a woman is battered. Domestic Violence is the leading cause of injury to women more than car accidents, muggings, and rapes combined... Nearly 1 in 5 teenage girls who have been in a relationship said a boyfriend threatened violence or self-harm if presented with a breakup. As many as 800 women are attacked during a 2-hour television program. It is reported that one in every three women will be battered in their lifetime."* (You can find more information at: https://domesticviolencestatistics.org/domestic-violence-statistics/)

It's no wonder women have struggled with identity, self-image and esteem issues for so long.

A poor self-image leads to an impulsive and competitive spirit. This is where we respond to life circumstances with a knee jerk reaction. We have no ability to determine for ourselves the best course of action because we care more about what people will think or say. We live to impress man. We look to others to determine our fate. We compare ourselves with others and feel inadequate. We feel like we don't match up and fail in sameness with them. Our image is healed in the mirror reflection (likeness, image, duplication, expression), of God's word.

The Apostle Paul warns against comparison saying:

> *"For we dare...compare ourselves with some that commend themselves: But they measuring themselves by themselves, and comparing themselves among themselves, are not wise."* 2 Corinthians 10:12 (KJV)

We find the solution to this deceptive practice in 2 Corinthians 3:18 where Paul also says: *"But we all, with open face beholding as in a glass (mirror) the glory of the Lord, are changed(transformed, altered, improved), into the same image from glory to glory, even as by the Spirit of the Lord."* (KJV)

The more we behold the face of Christ, the more we see ourselves in His image and likeness. Comparing ourselves with others leaves us feeling small and devalued. Looking in the mirror of God's word is equal to looking into the face of Jesus. In doing so, our hearts are healed, our mind is renewed and we are transformed into His resemblance.

Abuse was never God's intent for the woman.

"And the Lord God said, "It is not good that man should be alone (abandoned, deserted, isolated); I will make him a "helper comparable" to him." Gen.2: 18 (NKJ)

Synonyms for *"Comparable"* are: suitable, of equivalent quality - equivalent in character, form or function, as good as, equal to, in the same class, on a level with…

Adam said, *"She shall be called 'woman,' for she was taken out of man."* (Genesis 2:23 NKJ)

Ishshah is the Hebrew word for 'woman'. God fashioned or formed the rib which He had taken from the man into a woman. That declaration in itself is simply amazing. He then presented her to Adam and he called her *"bone of my bone and flesh of my flesh"*, because she came out of his own body. He distinguished, classified and celebrated her as 'Woman'.

Likewise, the definition of Ishshah is: Woman, Feminine, Female, Gentle and soft; Delicate--Exquisitely Fine, Dainty, and Pleasant to the Senses in a Soft, Mild, or Subtle Way...

As I continued to break down the meaning of each word and their various definitions, I found the following descriptions interesting: Easily Damaged, Fragile, and Requiring Tact in Handling. She's Ticklish, Finely Sensitive in Response, Tactful, Considerate and Charming.

This description brings Psalm 139: 13 – 18 to mind:

> *"You made all the delicate, inner parts of my body and knit them together in my mother's womb. Thank you for making me so wonderfully complex! It is amazing to think about. Your workmanship is marvelous—and how well I know it. You were there while I was being formed in utter seclusion! You saw me before I was born and scheduled each day of my life before I began to breathe. Every day was recorded in your book! How precious it is, Lord, to realize that you are thinking about me constantly! I can't even count how many times a day your thoughts turn toward me. [a] and when I waken in the morning, you are still thinking of me!"* (TLB)

You are God's Master Creation!

God possesses our reins. He controls our bridle, our passageway in life, our harnesses or advances. His eyes saw our substance being yet formed. When there were no days yet fashioned for us, in His book they were all written. Yes! We are fearfully and wonderfully made.

God 'formed' man and 'created' or 'fashioned', the woman. In each case, we see how God gave individual and specific detailed attention to His creation.

The woman is suited to be a helpmate, one who is capable to aid and assist man's needs and accomplishments. She came from his side representing her position in this astonishing matrimonial relationship.

Why the Rib?

Why did God take a rib from Adams side to fashion the woman you may ask?

The rib is amazingly essential. It appears that the rib possesses all the properties needed to equip and finalize the character, attributes and make-up of the woman. These enable her to fulfill the God-given purpose for her life.

I find it interesting that the birthing of Eve came from Adam's side requiring the shedding of blood. Similarly, when a woman gives birth to her children, from her body comes, water and blood. Blood in the bible is associated with covenant and life. Water also represents Life.

In addition, Christ gave life to His bride on the cross. The bible tells us that a soldier pierced Jesus in his side. Out came *"water and blood"*, thus the bride of Christ was born.

While the man slept, God opened his side and took out a rib. Adam and Eve entered into a covenant relationship that was established in blood shed from the man's own body.

Adam's declaration of the woman saying; *"she is bone of my bone and flesh of my flesh"* paints a beautiful picture of the closeness and union that can only be realized within the most intimate of relationships. The marriage covenant is a perfect joining together of heart, mind, soul and purpose.

The Similarities between the *"Rib"* and the *"Woman"*

First, science tells us that the rib wraps around the back and is connected to central nerves which send signals to the head. The woman is a covenant partner to her husband and has the exceptional ability to be the single most powerful and significant influence in his life. A wise husband values her opinion highly. However, the woman must be mindful to never use her influence to manipulate him for her own selfish motive.

Secondly, she is taken from the ribs, which is curvy in shape and surrounds the complete torso and protects the heart and all the vital organs in the body. A godly woman will seek to protect her husband's heart. She will keep his secrets and never expose his weaknesses.

Thirdly, like the marrow of the bone, she contains life-giving capability. She is equipped to receive the man's seed and present him with a child. Likewise, she incubates his dreams and his visions and labors over them prayerfully until fruition.

Fourth, the rib contracts and expands as we inhale and exhale. Similar to the rib, the woman possesses the ability to give and take. She is flexible and resilient, expandable yet sturdy.

Fifth, the rib cage supports and lifts the torso. Like the rib, the woman supports by lifting and holding her husband up through love, prayer, companionship and words of encouragement.

A man would never assault or abuse his own body. He would not purposely break his own ribs out of anger. He'd never divorce himself from his ribs. As a matter of fact, a man will go through every length to protect his body when participating in contact sports or performing dangerous tasks. He will be sure to wear protective gear to guarantee that he does not harm his ribs.

Reflections

Our Beginning Does Not Determine Our End
Chapter Five

1). **Paul warns against comparing ourselves among ourselves.**
    What solution does he offer in 2 Corinthians 3:18?

2). **Christ wants to be our Joy and our Song. He alone is our comfort and peace when we suffer great losses.**
    How has God proven to be your joy and your song in times of great loss? In what ways does He bring comfort to your soul?

3). **Have you ever been in a place so dark that it seemed there was no light to be found?**
    - *How did God turn your darkness into light?*
    - *How has God most spoken to you?*
    - *In what way do you hear His voice?*

4). **Point of Consideration or Discussion:**
    Have you ever wondered why God chose the Rib to make the woman? Review the similarities on the previous page for self-reflection or group discussion.

Scriptural Inheritance Affirmation:

"Oh, how can I give you up...? How can I let you go? How can I forsake you[a] My heart cries out within me; how I long to help you! No, I will not punish you as much as my fierce anger tells me to...For I am God and not man; I am the Holy One living among you, and I did not come to destroy." Hosea 11: 8-9 (TLB)

CHAPTER SIX

A Rock in a Hard Place

I would be remiss if I neglected to tell you about another very important member of the Zelophehad family. His name is, Gilead. Gilead is Hepher's father and Zelophehad's grandfather. Therefore, he is the great grandfather of Zelophehad's five daughters

NUM.27:1

Gilead's name means *"Rocky" or "Strong"* (New American Standard Bible – Open Edition)

He was a man of great valor. He knew no fear in the face of conflict.

Joshua 17:1 describes Gilead as *"a man of war"*. He was fearless and valiant. He possessed great boldness and confidence.

If we were to look back at our own families, chances are we will find in our genealogical background that there was someone like Gilead. Someone who was a rock in tough times, one who portrayed strength under pressure and one who was courageous and fearless.

Gilead was a man of war. He knew how to battle. Chances are he knew how to war prayerfully for his family as well.

The enemy would have us believe we come from a band of felons, crooks, offenders and thugs as if our destiny is predisposed for the same. While it is encouraging to find greatness in our posterity, it is more important to realize that we are born of God and for that reason, greatness lies within us. We are not defined by generational cycles of behavior nor the opinions and sentiments of others. We are who God says we are and can do what He says we can do.

Perhaps you are called to be the Rock in a hard place for your family.

See opposition as an occasion to trust God. Expect God to release generational blessings over you and your family. Determine to break generational curses by resisting former behavior and lifestyle choices. Pray and speak (proclaim or confess), the word of God over yourself and your loved ones. By doing this, we appropriate (adopt, seize or take) what God says and we make it our reality. Stop putting voice to what you see and begin to speak forth those things you do not yet see as though they already are. Remember, life and death is in the power of the tongue. Call your marriage blessed. Call your loved ones free from their addictions, repetitive incarcerations, vicious cycles of behavior and bondages. Call your body healed. Call peace to your troubled mind. Call calm to your run-away emotions.

In the face of trouble let Psalms 61:2 be your mantra – *"…I cry to you for help when my heart is overwhelmed. Lead me to the towering rock of safety."* (NLT)

Christ is our Rock. He is our Refuge and our Defense. Habitually in difficult times, God strategically places people in our lives that are also a rock to us. It could be a school teacher, neighbor, family friend, church leader or other.

When I was a young child, my grandmother and my mother were my *"Rock"*. They exhibited enormous strength and resilience in difficult times. They imparted in me a desire to know God and to seek after Him.

They both instilled in me and my brother's good morals, values, reverence for God and a great work ethic that has stuck with us all of our lives.

Maybe you are the one who is standing strong and who is praying for your loved ones to come to Christ. Be encouraged! God has called you out to be the one who will stand in the gap and build up the hedge around your loved ones. He hears your prayers and is working behind the scenes in the lives of each family member to bring them into the kingdom of God. It is His will that we and our whole house be saved.

Never underestimate the power of prayer

If you or someone you love is going through a hard time, like Zelophehad, call out to God.

His counsel may come unexpectedly, when least anticipated. It may happen while reading the word of God. It may happen during your time of worship. It could happen as a result of meeting a complete stranger, a casual acquaintance or even result from a song you hear. You may hear God speaking to you while reading this book. God knows how to get through to each one of us. His counsel and relief will always bring delight to our soul!

Living under the shadow of the Almighty

As you clearly know by now, Zelophehad's name means *"shadow of fear"*. However, his life was transformed when he took residence under the *"shadow of the Almighty"*.

When we are bombarded with fear, we need to make God our dwelling place.

> *Psalm 91:1 "Those who live in the shelter of the Most High will find rest in the shadow of the Almighty." (NLT)*

To move from the *"Shadow of Fear"*, you too will need to take new residence under the *"shadow of the Almighty"*. We must make the presence of God our habitation.

A secret place is not a covert, cloak-and-dagger, hole-and-corner. It is a place where our fears subside; our anxieties cease, troubles vanish and all the things that once disturbed us now come to a complete calm. Everything becomes silent, still and peaceful. Most secret places are restricted, confidential and private. The secret place of the Most High is open, available and accessible to all who will call upon the name of the Lord.

> *I'm reminded of Genesis 3: 9-11: ""...But the LORD God called to the man, "Where are you?" He answered, "I heard you in the garden, and I was afraid because I was naked; so I hid." And he said, "Who told you that you were naked?"" (NIV)*

Two great questions: *"Where are you?"* and *"Who told you that...?"* Many of us go into hiding because somebody told us we weren't good enough. We hear the voice of destiny calling but we fear because of prior personal immoral or unethical practices. We feel degraded and contaminated. Guilt and shame overtake us. We avoid God's presence because we feel unworthy. Are you in hiding? Your dilemma is no surprise to God. It's time you come out of obscurity and into the marvelous light of God's glory. Live your life deliberately. Seek God with intent. Look to your future with resolve. Step out with determination and commitment. Direct your focus on the goals, dreams and visions that are in your heart. Fix your eyes on Him who gave your life and know that He will lead your steps. Aim for the prize of fulfilling your objectives. Step out of the shadows of pain and into your purpose. Step out from obscurity to Destiny, from misery to History and from observation to Destination. Respond to the Call of God!

Typically, in times of trouble we don't feel like praying. We don't feel like reading the Bible. We don't feel like listening to worship music or attending church. Sometime the voice of the enemy is so loud that we listen to his lies and get even more depressed. We can't afford to allow our feelings to dictate our response to trouble. God's Word is Life and Peace. Run to it!

David said, *"My tears have been my meat day and night, while they continually say unto me, where is thy God?"* Psalm 42:3 (KJV)

Though many taunted him David abided in his secret place. He got lost in praises to His God.

Later in verse 5, David speaks to his soul - *"Why art thou cast down, O my soul? And why art thou disquieted in me? Hope thou in God: for I shall yet praise him for the help of his countenance."*

You too can learn how to find your secret place in Christ when your soul is disquieted (a feeling of anxiety or uneasiness), within you.

Zelophehad's shadow was not one of comfort, rest or protection. His was one of darkness and fear.

A *"Shadow"* is a resemblance, likeness, similarity of something

A shadow appears when rays from a source of light are blocked by an object. Fear is the object that blocked the light of God in Zelophehad's life. Fear casts a shadow and distorts our view of life. The enemy uses fear to block the light of God's presence. When this happens, it throws a shadow over our lives causing us to feel separated, alienated and far from God. However, the truth is that God will never leave us nor forsake us. The scripture tells us that while we were separated and alienated from God, He sent His son, the 'light' of the world to dispel the darkness and free us from our sin.

God said that even our darkness would be as a light unto Him.

The enemy will try to isolate us from other believers and good friends; He tries to stop us from attending church, reading the word of God, spending time in fellowship, and even tries to keep us from individual or corporate worship. Where there is darkness, the enemy has a legal right to operate. His desire is to keep us in the darkness. Jesus came to bring us out of darkness and into His marvelous light.

Fear causes a sense of alarm, danger, a feeling of concern, dread, anxiety, fright or a state of extreme apprehension. The Bible tells us that fear produces torment. Fear will cause us to panic and make wrong choices. Fear will hinder us from receiving the blessings of God and deprive us from our inheritance in Christ.

Clearly this spirit of fear does not come from God. God's light is fears antidote.

He promises that if we keep our mind on Him, He will keep us in perfect peace.

Perfect peace is flawless, unadulterated, unimpeachable, absolute, unqualified and whole.

Jesus introduces Himself as *"the light of the world"*

Walk in the Light

Jesus said: "I have come as a light into the world, that whoever believes in Me should not abide in darkness." John 12:46 (NKJ)

Jesus is The Great Physician. He has provided the remedy for fear. It is the light of His presence.

Jesus said to *"Walk in the Light"*. We cannot walk in light and darkness or faith and fear at the same time.

Fear causes us to look constantly behind us, looking dreadfully over our shoulder.

Light illuminates our path and shows us the way. When we are walking in the light, we are looking to God's promises with hope and expectation. Light expels darkness. Though the storms of life will rage against us, He will not abandon us as an orphan in the storm. Even there His light will lead us safely out of the storm.

> *1 Peter: 2: 9-10 says; "But you are the ones chosen by God, chosen for the high calling of priestly work, chosen to be a holy people, God's instruments to do his work and speak out for him, to tell others of the night-and-day difference he made for you—from nothing to something, from rejected to accepted."(MSG)*

Peter gives us seven valid points: *1) We are (Chosen) for the high calling of priestly work, 2.) (chosen) to be a holy people, 3) (chosen) to be God's instruments to do his work, 4) (chosen) to speak out for him, 5) (chosen), to tell others of the night-and-day difference he made for us, 6) (chosen), from nothing to something, 7) (chosen) from rejected to accepted."*

We have been specially selected, elected, preferred and hand-picked. Our purpose, destiny and reason for existence are rolled up in this one verse. We have been chosen individually, exclusively and absolutely!

In Times of Fear we have these Promises

- God will protect us (Genesis 15:1)
- God will not forget us (Isaiah 49:15)
- God strengthens us (Psalms 46:1-3)
- We do not need to fear darkness or violence (Psalms 91:5)
- We do not need to fear bad news (Psalms 112:7)
- Love drives fear away (1 John 4:18)

We Dwell in Safety & Security in Christ.

Safety has to do with the present while security has to do with the future.

Fear comes to rob us of our present and our future, but God assures us that both are securely in His hands.

Fear violated the lives of Zelophehad and his daughters and tried to steal their destiny and inheritance. Their history did not hinder them from fulfilling their destiny. When they stood at the Tabernacle entrance and requested their inheritance, they were securing both, their future and the future of many women to come.

I lived in fear's grip for most of my early life. I was mentally harassed, intimidated and dominated by fear.

Consequently, while living under the shadow of fear, I began to cling to the following scripture with its promises. All it takes is one verse that speaks to your life to sustain you.

Now let's look at this amazing scripture in Isaiah 43: 5-19 (NIV). These excerpts have become my go to safety net and is compatible to Isaiah 41: 10-13.

- Fear not I have redeemed you
- Fear not I have called you
- Fear not I will be with you
- Fear not I am the Lord your God
- Fear not I have ransomed you
- Fear not I have honored you
- Fear not I have loved you
- Fear not I will bless your children
- Fear not I have created you for my glory
- Fear not I have formed you
- Fear not I have made you
- Fear not I have chosen you
- Fear not I have declared, saved and proclaimed (announced, broadcasted) you)
- Fear not I work and who will reverse it
- Fear not I am King
- Fear not I make a way in the sea and a path through the mighty waters
- Fear not I delivered you from your enemies
- Fear not I will do a new thing
- Fear not I will make a road in the wilderness and rivers in the desert

"Fear not, I will" ...

These scripture verses reveal God's character and nature as well as His ability to perform. In them He demonstrates His absolute love for us. Here He declares what He has done for us, who He is to us, and what He will do for us. Because we have these precious promises, He commands us to: *"Fear not".*

We receive these promises by faith. Sometime ago, I was struggling to understand faith. I was seeking to better comprehend its meaning and how to activate it. Happily, I stumbled onto this amazing definition: Faith – *"the knowledge of God."*

It doesn't get any simpler than that. Faith is *"having the knowledge of God".* The more we develop the knowledge of who God is; the more our faith grows. We gain this knowledge by personal experience as well as hearing the word of God. Encounters with God reveal His power and His word reveals His promises.

An intimate knowledge of His nature, character and attributes, result in absolute confidence that He is who He said He is and will do what He said He will do.

> *Hebrews 11: 29-35 tells us: "By faith (the knowledge of God), they passed through the Red Sea as by dry land… By faith (the knowledge of God), the harlot Rahab did not perish…through faith (the knowledge of God), subdued kingdoms…quenched the violence of fire, escaped the edge of the sword, out of weakness were made strong, became valiant in battle, turned to flight the armies of the aliens…(by the knowledge of God), women received their dead raised to life again…"*

Reflections

A Rock in a Hard Place
Chapter Six

1). Can you think of one particular family member or friend who was a rock for you or stood strong in difficult times as a role model or godly example?

> *How did they inspire you by their example? What impression did they leave on your life?*

2). God ask Adam two great questions:
- "Where are you?"

> *Take a moment to consider where you are right now in your relationship with Christ and identify how you might advance your relationship.*

- B). "Who told you that?"

> *Who told you that you weren't good enough, strong enough, pretty enough, smart enough, couldn't make it and so on? Identify the steps you took or might take to eradicate the lies of the enemy.*

3). Do you have one favorite scripture verse that has become your go to scripture when opposition comes?

> *Share in group or think about it as you reflect on its ability to bring you peace in the midst of opposition.*

Scriptural Inheritance Affirmation:

"But I came by and saw you there, helplessly kicking about in your own blood. As you lay there, I said, 'Live!' And I helped you to thrive like a plant in the field. You grew up and became a beautiful jewel... So I wrapped my cloak around you to cover your nakedness and declared my marriage vows. I made a covenant with you, says the Sovereign Lord, and you became mine." Ezekiel 16: 6-8 (NLT)

CHAPTER SEVEN

A Crown of Glory & A Royal Diadem

Whether we are in good times or bad, during highs or lows of life; we can 'do' (accomplish, achieve, execute and perform "all things through Christ".

PHIL. 4:13

Whenever we are experiencing difficult circumstances, we can get through them because of and through Christ. We cannot trust our own strength or abilities. We cannot survive difficulty alone, but we are capable through Christ. It is by means of His strength and empowerment working in us. You can do all things through Christ who strengthens, equips and qualifies you. When we suffer opposition, affliction and great turmoil in life, we cope with it through Christ who enables or assists us.

The definition of *"Through"* is: by way of, by means of, as a result of, from start to finish, allowing unobstructed or unhindered passage: Therefore in the midst of trials we can say…

- I can do all things 'by way of Christ', which strengthens me.
- I can do all things 'by means of Christ', which strengthens me.
- I can do all things 'as a result of Christ', which strengthens me.
- I can do all things 'from start to finish', because of Christ, who strengthens me.
- I can do all things, 'through unobstructed or unhindered passage', because of Christ, who strengthens me.

Fear attempts to keep us from accomplishing dreams and visions because we are made to feel weak, inferior and incapable.

Called by a New Name

The daughters of Zelophehad had a secure identity. Our identity (individuality, uniqueness, qualities, character, personality), is not based on our accomplishments, level of income or other resources derived from this world's standard. We must develop an identity based on who God says we are and from a personal relationship with Christ. Each of us are unique individuals; distinct in character, nature, qualities and personality. We are exclusively and exceptionally created. We are rare and unlike any other. We are created for His glory and for His pleasure.

Isaiah 62: 2-5 tells us that we are called by a *"new name"*.

> *"...you will be called by a new name that the mouth of the Lord will bestow. You will be a crown of splendor in the Lord's hand, a royal diadem in the hand of your God. No longer will they call you Deserted, or name your land Desolate. But you will be called Hephzibah, [a] and your land Beulah[b] for the Lord will take delight in you,*

and your land will be married. As a young man marries a young woman, so will your Builder marry you; as a bridegroom rejoices over his bride, so will your God rejoice over you." (NIV)

This new name is one which the Lord has 'designated' (chosen, selected, assigned, allocated and preferred) for us.

We are "a crown of glory" in His hand.

Isaiah 62: 3 says: "Thou shalt also be a crown of glory in the hand of the LORD, and a royal diadem in the hand of thy God." (NKJV)

We are *"in the hand of the Lord"*, under His protection, power and influence. He holds us proudly as a *"crown of glory"*. He chose us to represent His beauty, splendor, brilliance and magnificence in the earth. We are the height of His radiance. He created us in His own image.

Additionally, we are considered a (royal) 'diadem' of beauty. A diadem is a *"headdress" or a "tiara"*.

According to Wikipedia a diadem is a type of crown, specifically an ornamental headband worn by Eastern monarchs and others as a 'badge of royalty'. It is an emblem of regal power or dignity. The crown traditionally represents power, 'legitimacy', victory, triumph, honor and glory, as well as righteousness and resurrection.

Given such definitions, we can see how the royal diadem may very well denote our position in Christ. We have been given power over the enemy. We are legitimate heirs of God through the blood of Jesus and walk in victory and triumph. He has conferred honor upon us by making us His sons and daughters. He has made us the righteousness of God in Christ Jesus. Our past no longer pronounces judgment over our destiny or assesses our value. The blood of Jesus has paid in full the cost that purchased our salvation and we are redeemed from the charges that were held against us. Satan no longer lords mastery over us. His powers are broken and Jesus Christ is Lord.

> *Isaiah 62 verse 4 tells us: "You shall no longer be termed Forsaken, [b] Nor shall your land any more be termed Desolate; [c] But you shall be called [d] Hephzibah, and your land [e]Beulah; For the Lord delights in you, And your land shall be married." (NKJV)*

You shall no longer be termed (called) 'forsaken' or 'disowned'.

The definition for *"termed" is actually "defined"*

You are no longer considered abandoned, rejected, jilted, discarded or disowned. Neither are you defined by your encounter of being deserted, forsaken, unproductive, unfruitful or infertile. You are no longer forbidden or unwelcomed - but are completely accepted and embraced in the presence of God. You are no longer looked upon as dejected, wretched or miserable. You have been far removed from all depression, sorrow and mournfulness. No longer are you inconsolably grief-stricken, despairing or heartbroken. These things shall no longer be your identity.

You are no longer defined, (described, classified, identified or characterized), by your past experiences, failures, previous lifestyle choices, sinful behavior, ungodly conduct or influences.

God Loves Us Too Much to Let Us Go

Our circumstance does not define our final outcome. Our past does not define our future. And haters do not define our significance or value.

This world's system does not define our success. The doctor's report does not define the number of our days. Our income does not define our true wealth. Where we live does not define where we will go in life.

We have a new name. We are called; Healed, Redeemed, Blessed, Favored, Beloved, Delivered, Forgiven, Righteous, More than Conquerors, Triumphant, Victors and not victims, Strong and not weak, Above only, and not beneath, The Apple of His Eye, Royalty, Sons and Daughters of the Most High God - When someone calls you out of your name, Answer only to your New Name!

Your name shall be *"Hephzi-bah"*.
Hephzi-bah means *"Delight"*, which signifies enjoyment, pleasure, happiness, joy, amusement, and satisfaction.

God Himself relishes over you. He celebrates you. He dances over you with song. He is radically in love with you and receives great pleasure and joy when you come into His presence. That's a new revelation for most of us to realize that God loves us that much. He delights over you!

He goes on the say, *"As the bridegroom rejoices over his bride, so does the Lord rejoice over you"*. Wow! That's a powerful statement and reveals a love that is overwhelmingly breathtaking. God is in covenant with us, like a husband is in covenant with his wife.

As one who rejoices, He stands up and spins like a top over you. You cause the Most High to twirl at your presence.

Furthermore, you shall be called *"Beulah"--"Thou art married."*

This verse confirms that (through Christ), God has entered into a binding marriage covenant with us.

When we receive Christ into our hearts, we go from 'forsaken' to 'beloved bride' and the blessings of the Kingdom of God are ours to enjoy.

Verse 6 tells us more: *"Thy "builder" or "restorer,"* that is, God;

As builder, He is our creator, maker and designer. He builds us up when life has torn us down. He refreshes us when we've become worn and weary from opposition. He is our producer, constructor and architect. He restores us!

As restorer, He is the one who maintains us. He renovates our hearts, minds and souls. He reconditions us and mends us. Like the potter's clay, He restores, renews and reforms our marred and broken vessels.

> **No matter how shattered our life becomes, He remains our "builder" and "restorer".**

God has restored or reinstated us to our original position with Him, through Christ. We have been bought back into a right relationship with Him.

I am both humbled and thrilled to have the privilege of entering into the presence of Almighty God. But I never realized that He is equally thrilled about my coming before Him.

Zephaniah 3:17 tells us: *"The Lord your God in your midst, The Mighty One, will save; He will rejoice over you with gladness, he will quiet you with His love, He will rejoice over you with singing."* (NKJV)

What a comfort to know that He is in our midst and with His love, He quiet's us. He serenades us with song. Additionally, He celebrates, cheers, exults, delights, is made glad, is pleased, takes pleasure in and joys over us. That's incredible!

Even more amazing: *"Rejoice"* is taken from two words –

"Re"- concerning, regarding, or with reference to

"Joice": To practice the act over and over again.

Imagine that! It's not just a one-night stand with Christ. Nor is it a one-sided celebration. But 'concerning, regarding or with reference to you', every time you enter His presence, He stands up and breaks into a song and dance repeatedly, over and over again.

Our Past Does Not Define Us!

I have used this phrase consistently throughout this book. It is important that we realize that we are not defined by anything or anyone. God defined us upon our creation. You are not labeled by man, but by God's description, purpose and destiny concerning you. You have His stamp of affirmation. He has already branded (named, identified, characterized) you.

In biblical times, a seal was used to guarantee security or indicate ownership. The Roman authorities used a seal to secure Jesus' tomb (Matt 27:66). Kings used a signet ring to stamp their decrees, which is also called a seal. The Holy Spirit seals those of us who trust in Christ. This seal (The Holy Spirit), is our guarantee that those who follow Christ are owned by him and secure in him.

Unfortunately, we tend to lose our identity in our career, marriage, economic status, motherhood, ministry and other self-promoting endeavors. However, if we lose either of these things - that which we've allowed to identify us no longer exists. As a result, we lose our sense of worth. We also sometimes lose our identity due to how someone else perceives us or how they treat us.

According to the Merriam-Webster dictionary, the word *"define"* means; to determine or identify the essential qualities or meaning of;

to explain the meaning of; to show or describe (someone or something) clearly and completely.

God as our Creator, defines us in His word. He describes we, who follow Him, as His sons and daughters in very delightful and loving terms as seen in previous and following chapters.

We must learn to decree over ourselves God's description and not words derived from what others say or do. If death and life are in the power of the tongue, then we must use it to declare blessing and not cursing over ourselves.

We are not held hostage to the wrong choices and decisions of our past. They cannot define who we are.

Consider the following bible characters that refused to allow circumstances or wrong choices to define them:

- *Esther was not defined by her Jewishness (Esther - chapters 1-10).*
- *Naomi was not defined by her widow status, loss of two sons and bitterness (Ruth – chapter 1).*
- *Gomer was not defined by her harlotry (Hosea – chapter 1).*
- *Rahab was not defined by her life of prostitution (Joshua – chapter 2).*
- *Peter was not defined by his denial of Christ (Matt. 26:31).*
- *The woman at the well was not defined by her multiple marriages (John:4)*
- *Abigail was not defined by her abusive husband (1 Samuel – chapter 25).*
- *Sara was not defined by her inability to bear children (Gen.18:11).*
- *The Daughters of Zelophehad were not defined by their history (Num. 26:33).*

For most of his life, Zelophehad was defined by his name (shadow of fear).

A new day dawned upon Zelophehad and his daughters. It was like coming out of darkness and into a marvelous light. He got back his joy. His peace was now restored. The chains of darkness were shattered.

A new day has dawned for you too. We must refuse to live under the dictate and rule of fear and the harassing memories of our past or even the concerns over our outcome in life. We can only move ahead by keeping our eyes on what lies before us.

We All Possess the Personality That Best Compliments Our Gift

Too often, our personality becomes marred by painful experiences. In Chapter four we talked about treasuring the gift that you are and each sister's contribution to the process. It seems the daughters of Zelophehad managed to protect their individuality despite their different temperaments.

Each sister contributed to the process and each temperament was vital to the plan. When working with others, it is important to know those who are around you and draw from the specific gift or strength that each one possesses. Many of us have not developed good self-awareness and unfortunately follow the path someone else laid out for us. As a result, we are not conscious or attentive to the gifts or abilities we possess. The Apostle Paul likens it to the physical body telling us; every joint supplies according to its designed function, therefore one is not more valuable than the other.

In any relationship, we would be wise to learn to delegate appropriate tasks to the individual who has the ability to best carry things out to completion and perfection, rather than place demand on someone who does not walk in that particular strength just because they are available. Even in a marriage, let the one who is more capable handle the finances, cooking or other responsibilities.

Release Unrealistic Demands and Expectations

If we seek God, He will show us how to combine our strengths and build on our weaknesses for the betterment of our relationships and the fulfillment of our destiny. Habitually relationships are ruined because we place unrealistic demands and expectations where they cannot be exercised. If we want a fulfilled marriage, business, career, ministry or other, we must release unrealistic demands and expectations. If we want to produce children who rely on God for guidance and counsel, we must instruct them early on to seek Him by means of prayer and reading His word. Placing unrealistic demands and expectations on them will only produce frustration and breached relationships. As they learn to seek counsel from God, He will reveal their gifts and expose their talents. We then can come alongside them and help exercise and develop them.

Zelophehad encouraged the strengths and gifts of his daughters. Their names may have derived from a father's initial experience, but each name also declared their destiny.

You may ask how that fits in relationship to the first two daughters whose name meant *"Disease" and "Trembling"*. That's a very good question.

Disease" and *"Trembling"* – These names merely identify a painful season associated with their father's life. Sometimes it's the ashes of our life, which produce our greatest potential and bring forth beauty beyond our greatest expectation.

A name not only declares our destiny but declares our victory. What we have come from is sometime as significant as what we will become.

Reflections

A Crown of Glory & a Royal Diadem
Chapter Seven

1). We can do, accomplish, complete, achieve, execute and perform all things through Christ.

> *What is it that you wish to do that you have not yet accomplished, completed, achieved, executed or performed and what steps do you think it will take to make it happen?*

2). We are no longer termed forsaken or disowned according to Isaiah 62: 4.

> *Have you ever felt forsaken? If so when did you come to realize that you are completely accepted by God?*

3). Life and death are in the power of the tongue.

> *How then can we appropriate into our lives what God says about us?*

4). No matter how shattered our life becomes, He remains our "builder" and "restorer".

> *Think about or share in group what this means to you.*

Scriptural Inheritance Affirmation:

"Can a woman forget her nursing child, that she should have no compassion on the son of her womb? Even these may forget, yet I will not forget you. Behold, I have engraved you on the palms of my hands..." Isaiah 49: 15-16 (ESV)

CHAPTER EIGHT

Five is the number of Grace

I do not believe it is coincidental that God gave Zelophehad five daughters. Five is the number for *"Grace"*.

The secular definition for Grace is elegance, refinement, beauty, style, poise and charm.

The daughters of Zelophehad apparently possessed them all. God gave them all the necessary attributes and characteristics they would need to fulfill their destiny.

However, on a spiritual note, Grace is also 'Divine Enablement'.

Through Jesus Christ, God divinely enabled us to become the sons and daughters of the Most High God. We are saved through 'divine enablement'.

We did nothing to earn, merit or indulge in such grace.

God also gave these sisters His Divine Enablement to carry out their assignment. They were thoroughly equipped. God's power rested upon them and the thing that seemed impossible became possible.

God has deposited dreams and visions in your heart too. If you will trust Him, He is well able to equip and enable you to fulfill your desires and achieve the impossible as well.

God had their back

The daughters of Zelophehad stood before Moses and the leaders with great confidence and expectation as they claimed their father's inheritance. We must do the same. God has given us great and precious promises, but we must lay hold of them by faith. There will always be obstacles, but He is an eternally present help, support and comfort in times of distress.

When Moses took the petition of these five sisters before God, His reply was, *"the daughters of Zelophehad are right."*

Because God's grace was upon them, He approved the daughters of Zelophehad and Moses granted them their request.

God alone graces us with the ability to step into our destiny

Frequently we are told that in order to reach our destiny, we must connect with the 'right' people, supposing that these people can help us accomplish our dreams and goals in life. While I don't disagree, in all actuality, it might be the people whom we cast aside or kick to the curb who are the ones most sufficient to aid and assist us. Even Jesus had His Judas, but Jesus called him friend. Many times, the one who challenges us or tests our character is who helps us the most. Left to ourselves, we will pick people based on outward appearance. Those who make us feel comfortable or secure or who appear to have the resources, titles, positions or connections.

My point is, while we should be selective, we are not always capable of choosing the 'right' people. God alone makes "divine connections". Unfortunately, when we put our trust in man, sadly, we often find that their support comes with strings attached. When God opens doors, makes connections and surrounds us with His divine favor, there are no strings attached. Only He knows the heart of man and knows who He has appointed to adjoin us in our destiny call.

Don't let circumstances or people label you.

Some will try to put labels on you. But you don't have to wear their labels. You've been branded, described, categorized and classified by your Father God. He calls you Holy, Righteous, All together lovely, Precious, Child of the Most High. He calls you Saved, Healed, Delivered, Set free, Made whole, Competent, Well able, Incredible and Complete. Like the labels on the back of a garment, that sometimes becomes a source of irritation, we must cut it off. Don't throw away the garment (dream, vision), just because of the label. Zelophehad's first two daughters were labeled Disease and Trembling, but when Zelophehad cried out to God, God destroyed their labels.

You are marked for favor, honor and success. Be mindful how you label yourself. Don't allow your experiences, failures or genealogies influence your identity or opinion of yourself. You are uniquely in a class all your own. You are refined with the elegance of God's glory. You have been made in His image and His likeness. You are a carrier of your Father's name. You possess His nature, character and attributes. Only walk in them habitually and each step becomes more natural as you do.

Don't Allow Your Past to Define You, Defy Your Past.

People will attempt to define us or brand us according to our past. In the natural, our brand is our 'trademark' which distinguishes us from others. It identifies us and includes our characteristics, talents, style, habits and tendencies. When people hear our name certain images or thoughts automatically come to mind. Our old life may have left us with a bad reputation. People may expect certain actions, attitudes or behavior based on our past. As we grow deeper in our relationship with Christ we progressively transform or converge into our new self. Where we once held specific views, opinions or carried ourselves in a particular contrasting manner, we no longer are that person. We are brand ambassadors for Christ. A brand ambassador is someone who represents and embodies the brand he or she is endorsing. Therefore, we are His representatives and are called to exemplify who He is to others. We are messengers of His love and conduits of His grace. We must learn to be consistent in portraying attributes and lifestyle choices that embody a Christ like representation.

I am reminded of how while working for a corporation the company experienced a rebranding due to changes concerning their name, business model and structure. This was necessary if they wanted to stay current technologically with the times. I had never heard of such thing and was astonished to witness the necessary steps to establish their new brand. They labored tenaciously to ensure that the brand accurately exemplified their ultimate objectives, vision, goals and purpose.

Before you set out to rebrand yourself, as Christ's ambassador, keep in mind that we represent and embody Him. Everything we do must endorse His message and exemplify His life. Therefore, we are His diplomats and are called to demonstrate who He is to others. Consider the same aspects in the previous paragraph. What is your dream or vision? The Bible tells us to write our vision down and make it plain so others can read it and help carry it to fruition (Habakkuk 2:2). What is your purpose and how do you plan to accomplish it? Do you have the resources? Do you possess the gift or talent that is required? Who is your audience? Most of all, is this your passion?

Do you sense God's leading? If so, allow Him to direct your path. If we get too caught up in trying to make our own name famous, we've only proven that our new brand is still all about us and not Christ. As followers of Christ, we should clearly identify the message or image we wish to project or portray before others. Not for vanity reasons, but to express Christ as His brand ambassadors. Ultimately, our goal should be to act as a representative or promoter of who He is and to tell others about the new man we've become through our relationship with Him.

> *2 Cor. 6:3 says: "We put no stumbling block in anyone's path, so that our ministry will not be discredited." (NIV)*

We help govern what others will think when they hear our name by the life we live and by the unswerving godly conduct and behavior we display. There is no guarantee that everyone will speak well of you no matter how you live. While we can't always control how others perceive us or what others say about us – in the end, we want to please God, have a clean conscience before Him and ultimately hear him say *"well done"*. Make every effort to decrease so that Christ may increase. Die to self, bury your past and live intentionally unto Christ daily.

Call forth those things that are not as though they already are

Scripture tells us to speak into our future. We are encouraged to call forth those things we desire as though they already exist. That doesn't mean we go around calling forth a new house, a new car, a big bank account and so on. These callings forth is not like pulling rabbits out of a hat or rubbing the magic lantern and having a genie pop out to grant us three wishes.

We read in Romans 4:17; *"And this promise is from God himself, who makes the dead live again and speaks of future events with as much certainty as though they were already past."* (TLB)
Therefore, we can speak to our future by calling forth those things that God promises according to His Word.

If we are sick, we can call forth healing because Jesus took our sicknesses and diseases upon His body and by His stripes we are healed (1 Peter 2:24).

If we are bound by the enemy, we can call forth our deliverance because Jesus came to set the captives free - defeating the enemy on the cross.

> *Col. 1:13-14 "For he has rescued us from the dominion of darkness and brought us into the kingdom of the Son he loves, in whom we have redemption, the forgiveness of sins." (NIV)*

The thing we call forth must be supported by scripture or else it's merely psychic or soulish in nature.

Just as we can call forth those things that are not yet manifest into our future, by declaration of faith, we can speak victory to our past.

Tell your past that Jesus has cast your sins into the sea of forgetfulness. Jesus remembers them no more and neither should you. Forget those dead things (mistakes, faults, failures, disappointments, wrong choices, etc.), of the past and call forth the life-giving promises of God. When those dead things come to shore, throw them back into the sea. You are a new creation in Christ Jesus. Call forth your inheritance, call forth your destiny and call forth your pending favorable outcome!

Defy means to; challenge, resist, and disregard.

So challenge your past with the word of God. Resist it by walking freely and confidently in your new life in Christ. Disregard it and consider your past as a debt paid in full.

Destiny is calling

Joseph survived the pit and the prison because he heard Destiny's call in a dream.

Naomi and Ruth survived the death of their loved ones. There is no indication that they actually heard Destiny's call; it appears that they more or less stumbled onto the path of destiny with their decision to return to Bethlehem. God often leads us through the Holy Spirit unaware to our natural senses.

Zelophehad survived the shadow of fear because he cried out to God and Destiny showed up in his daughters.

The daughters of Zelophehad survived in a culture that demeaned them just because they were women. They sensed Destiny igniting a flame on the inside and consequently, they became exasperated concerning the injustice regarding the laws of inheritance.

Destiny may call in different ways. God may use various methods and means to gently nudge you. It may be a dream, a simple decision, the result of a hearts cry, or the igniting of a flame within. However, you can be sure Destiny awaits you. You were created with purpose. You were fashioned with intention. Your life has definite meaning, purpose, substance and value.

The Potter's Clay

Our history does not have the ability to abort God's purpose concerning us. As declared earlier, He will take those things that the enemy meant for evil and cause them to work for our good. The things we thought would destroy us can actually catapult us into God's destiny for our lives.

> *Isaiah 29:16 says, "Surely your turning of things upside down shall be esteemed as the potter's clay:" (KJV)*

Your problem is nothing more than clay in the potter's hand. Your financial problem is just clay, your troubled marriage is just clay, your prodigal children are just clay, that job situation, ministry opposition, or business challenge is just clay. Your health issues are just clay in the hands of the Potter.

Whatever you're experiencing, it's just clay. God can take, mold and shape it into something spectacular.

Violated (vs) Validated

As a little girl, when my father left our family, I felt abandoned. I felt violated because someone or something had taken my father's affections from us. A series of other events occurred in my life that made me feel further violated. It seemed as if I was in a perpetual whirlwind spiraling downward.

My hopes and dreams were diminished. All these things made me feel devalued, unfit, and ashamed.

However, when I received Christ into my heart, my life seemed to take a turn onto a new path. I gradually began to feel loved, cherished, honored, valued, significant and esteemed. In time, I began to see myself through His eyes and not the eyes of my wretched past.

I often think about how Gomer (in the book of Hosea), must have felt when her illicit affairs ended tragically with her standing as a slave on an old rundown auction block. She stood there filled with shame, guilt and condemnation, thinking her life was surely over. Who could ever love her now? Suddenly she heard a distinctive voice among the bidding and the quiet chatter of those standing around. Looking up, she saw a familiar silhouette walking into the crowd. The people parted as they quickly made pathway for the unexpected bidder. As he made his way forward, Gomer recognized the frame and stature to be that of her beloved husband, Hosea. How could this be possible? She continued to observe as he reached the platform. Finally, she wiped her tear-filled eyes and looked up, gazing into his tender countenance. He had come to redeem her. His eyes were filled with love and compassion for Gomer. He purchased Gomer and took her home to her children. When they got home, she began to call him, 'My Master'. Hosea sat her down and knelt before her and said, do not call me *"My Master"*. *Though he had gained legal ownership of her, he said to her, call me "My husband"*. (Hosea 2: 16)

Hosea honored the covenant relationship that the two of them entered into. He treated Gomer as if she never abandoned their marriage bed for another. He restored her to her children as their faithful mother. Her past did not determine her destiny nor did her present circumstances dictate her future. Her end was greater than her beginning. Unaware to her, the thing she sought after was there all the time.

This is a picture of God's love for us. He sent His Son to die for us so that we would be redeemed (to regain ownership of). The meaning of Hosea's name is *"Redeemer"*.

Jesus purchased us back at great expense and looks upon us as if we never sinned.

Sin violated us but God validated us through his son, Jesus Christ.

We were lost but now we are found, blinded by sin and alienated from God but now bought back again.

We were bound for an eternal hell but now on our way to heaven for all eternity where there will be no more sorrow. No more pain. No more crying. All tears will be wiped away from our eyes. We will then behold the face of our 'Redeemer'.

Furthermore, we have the promise of an abundant life here on earth blessed with God's favor and mercy. We will suffer some difficulties in this life, but He promised to be with us to deliver us out of (though not always from), them all.

God never gives up on us. Like Hosea pursued Gomer, Christ pursues us. In the same way as Gomer, we too must respond to His relentless love without hesitation.

Sin left us like Gomer, standing on the slave block waiting for the next bidder to purchase our soul, only to look up and see Jesus walking through the crowd of bidders coming to lay claim on us with the price of His own blood. His love led us to repentance. I'm so grateful for the mercy and grace He lavished upon us. Truly His love is without limits; it knows no boundaries and is free from all restrictions.

The Power of Soul Ties

The daughters of Zelophehad were successful in reaching their destiny because they walked in the power of agreement. Their hearts were knitted together in covenant relationship.

Unfortunately, many are connected to their past through soul ties. Their soul is still connected emotionally to someone of the past. Memories haunt them and attempt to allure and entice them. They feel like something is missing and long to have what they believe they've either lost or have been deprived of. A soul tie is the counterfeit for covenant.

Soul ties are established through intimate experiences (rather sexual or emotional), or pledges of commitment and dedication. It can be a first love you just can't seem to get over or resulting from a relationship where you made an allegiance. We swear to someone that we will *"never"* love another and take no thought to the binding effects of those words.

The daughters of Zelophehad experienced a joining together that was ordained by God. Their relationship was deeply associated with their destiny.

Please note the vast difference between a soul tie and a covenant. The best illustration of a covenant, other than the one we have with Christ, is that of a husband and wife. The bible tells us that the two shall become one flesh. They enter into a covenant before God. The physical consummation further ties the two together as one in holy matrimony. Contrariwise, when a person has ungodly sexual relations or emotional affairs with another person, an ungodly soul tie is formed. This unholy allegiance serves only to fulfill the flesh.

Breaking Soul Ties

Promises that fit the description of vows, commitments, allegiances and agreements to another in the form of a soul tie hold you hostage. Should the relationship end, you can be left with a gaping emotional wound. You may try to move on but continue to be plagued by beguiling thoughts of the person with whom you have entered into a sexual, verbal or emotional soul tie.

To break a soul tie one must submit to the Lordship of Jesus Christ - asking Him to come into your heart. Repent of any sins committed that may have forged the soul tie, such as sexual sins or an unreasonable vow. Get rid of gifts, pictures or other objects that may serve as constant reminders. Refuse to have any association with the individual and verbally renounce any allegiance that opened the door to the soul tie, in Jesus Name. Break free from your emotional past (people, places and objects).

2 Corinthians 10:3-6 tells us to break free from mental strongholds (thoughts, images and toxic memories). Break free from the bondages of guilt shame and condemnation associated with former allegiances.

If we are going to pursue the destiny God has for us, it will require the breaking of soul ties and the disposal of toxic relationships. I hope the following scripture will help you understand this truth.

> *1 Corinthians 6:15-17 says: "Do you not know that your bodies are members of Christ? ...Or do you not know that he who is joined to a harlot is one body with her? ...But he who is joined to the Lord is one spirit with Him." (NKJ)*

Reflections

Five is the Number of Grace
Chapter Eight

1). God gave the daughters of Zelophehad His Divine Enablement to carry out their assignment. God's power rested upon them and the thing that seemed impossible became possible.

Can you remember a time when you thought there was no way you could possibly do or accomplish something only to find that God graced you for the task?

2). God sends people into our lives to aide and assist us on our destiny journey. It is important to recognize that left to ourselves we would choose people based on our own intellect.

- *Who has God graced to be in your life to help develop you for your destiny?*
- *How have they most influenced the outcome of your destiny?*

3). The daughters of Zelophehad survived in a culture that demeaned them just because they were women. They sensed Destiny stirring them on the inside and consequently, they became exasperated concerning the injustice regarding the laws of inheritance.
Two questions:

- *How do you sense destiny stirring inside you?*
- *And what exasperates (frustrates, annoys) you to the point that you wish you could change it?*

Scriptural Inheritance Affirmation:

Because the Sovereign Lord helps me, I will not be disgraced. Therefore, I have set my face like a stone, determined to do his will. And I know that I will not be put to shame... See, the Sovereign Lord is on my side! Who will declare me guilty?

ISAIAH 50: 7 (NLT)

CHAPTER NINE

A Gateway of Hope

We talked about Hosea and Gomer in the previous chapter. I want to take a moment to bring out some other vital facts from this story that so beautifully coincides with our theme.

Many times, we fall into bondage and think there is no way out. These verses give us hope. Just like Hosea allured Gomer back to him as her husband, God will allure you back to Himself. He will draw you back through the power of His amazing steadfast love.

> *Hosea 2: 15 "... I will return her vineyards to her and transform the Valley of Trouble into a gateway of hope." (NLT)*

> *It goes on to say; "She will give herself to me there, as she did long ago when she was young, when I freed her from her captivity in Egypt."*

God turned things around for Gomer. Sadly, we too have given ourselves away in search to find the same worth Gomer longed for. We've tried multiple paths, yet none satisfied. We too have played the harlot.

However, there is no life that can't be transformed by God when it is yielded to Him. He will turn things around for you too.

Gomer did not decide on a life of harlotry. She didn't sell her body for money like a prostitute. Instead, driven by her pain, she offered herself in search for love.

When our life, our marriage, our family, our health or finances are in the Valley of Achor (Trouble), God will give us a door of hope, a gateway of deliverance. He will cause us to sing again and to lie down in safety.

Gomer represents Israel in this story. Though God said He would punish Israel for going after other gods and forgetting Him, He later said He would *"allure"* her and bring her into the wilderness where He would speak comfortably unto her. To allure is to attract, appeal, pull or draw. Your wilderness is often a place of God's visitation and your transformation.

Another term used for allure is *"entice"*. God loves us so much that He is willing to provide the incentive to motivate us to call out to Him.

The very term *"allure"* is a word used in the language of love. It is the same language that Hosea used to allure Gomer when she went astray and sought other lovers.

He provided the incentive for her to return when he continued to cherish the children she left behind. He also anonymously purchased precious gifts that he knew she loved and enjoyed, but her lovers could not or would not provide them for her.

Subsequently, he walked into the courtyard where she was being sold as a slave and bid until the required price to purchase Gomer's freedom was reached. You may recall that in this redemption, Hosea determined that she would not return to him as a slave but instead he would restore her as his beloved wife.

Just as God did Israel, Hosea said: *"I will lead her into the wilderness and speak comfortably unto her."*

God leads us to a quiet place and speaks words of comfort, hope and love. He doesn't remind us of our infidelities or rehearse despicable past behavior. Instead, He said, *"I will give her a door of hope for the Valley of Achor."*

He will transform the Valley of Trouble into an expectation of hope.

The Valley of Achor signifies a valley filled with worry, distress, anxiety, care, suffering, woe and concern. It is a place of strife, unrest, disorder, disturbance, turmoil and conflict. This is not where God wants you to dwell. He is lifting you up and out of the low places of your life.

Even when the Valley of Trouble is the result of our own choices, God will faithfully draw us back to Himself and give us a door of hope. Our sufferings will never be able to exceed God's ability to deliver.

When we don't know who we are, devastation is inevitable. Gomer's name actually means 'Complete'. Because Gomer didn't know that she was 'Complete', she lived a life of brokenness and misery. She tried to fill her empty soul in search for love, acceptance, significance and approval.

God goes on to promise to restore our song and our dance as in our youth.

You will not call me *"my Master"*, but instead will call me, *"my Husband"*. Only in Christ can we find this kind of restoration. He enters into a covenant of safety and betrothal (marriage) forever. We, who were far off, can experience a relationship of righteousness (just as if we never strayed), loving kindness, faithfulness, mercy and intimacy with God.

He has given us a Door of Hope for the Valley of Trouble. Jesus said: *"I am the door. If anyone enters by me, He will be saved…"* John 10:9 (NKJV).

God is a God of Mercy

Gomer gave birth to three children in her marriage to Hosea. Each child's name was associated with God's plan for Israel's intended punishment. Instead God determined that in His mercy, *"I will say to those called 'Not my people,' 'You are my people'; and they will say, 'You are my God'"* (Hosea 2:23 NIV). This clearly illustrates God's infinite love for you and I, who were not His people but now have become His people.

Our Future is Secure in Christ.

Like Zelophehad, many fear the future. Our outlook is frequently grimly influenced by our past. We find assurance in the following promises:

- God has plans for our future (Jer. 29:11)
- God will bless our future if we obey Him (Deut. 5:29)
- Do not plan your future like evil people (Jer. 10:2-3)
- God gives us hope for our future (Jer. 31:17)
- God prepares us for the future (1 Cor. 2:9)

We can learn many lessons from Our Past.

The daughters of Zelophehad taught us that our end is not determined by our beginning.

- We must set our gaze firmly on the course before us and refuse to look behind us in order to reach our destination without wavering.
- We must persistently keep our pace with determination and endurance.
- We must be tenacious in our faith. Holding firmly to the promises of God, and not be easily pulled away from our goals.
- We must be willing to give up something in order to achieve something more vital and make pleasing God our highest priority.

The thing we suffer is the very thing that will thrust us into the divine plan, purpose and destiny that God has for us. Our afflictions are considered light and momentary when compared to eternity. They actually will produce for us and not render a verdict contrary to the plan God has concerning us. Our oppositions will generate a far more exceeding and eternal weight of glory, both now and eternally.

After we have come through, our pain is transformed into passion and our passion drives our every ambition to reach others.

Passion becomes the motivating ambition that forces us into our destiny and arouses every determination and impulse.

Destiny will use what seems insignificant in your life to get you where you fear you will never go and accomplish what you dread will never come to pass.

Destiny Will Choose What Others Reject

Destiny will cause your past to connect with your future in a positive way. It must have been difficult for the daughters of Zelophehad to attend the census meeting in the tabernacle knowing that the law of inheritance disqualified them from receiving any distribution of property from their deceased father (Num. 27: 1-7). However, destiny chooses what others reject. They went with determination, focus and commitment. They were driven by persistence, purpose and passion. The actual thing that they had been denied became the driving force that propelled them forward.

The precise thing we count as a crisis in our lives is the exact thing that God uses as an opportunity for our deliverance or victory. In turn, our deliverance or victory opens the way of deliverance or victory for others and sometimes for future generations.

Exposing False Entitlement

They patiently waited out the census process and at a convenient time, they approached Moses, Eleazar, the leaders and the entire congregation.

The shadow of fear had vanished from their lives. Not a trace of its evil influence remained. They were free from the limitations, restrictions and barriers of fear. Now, instead of fear, they possessed confidence, boldness and assurance.

> *Scripture tells us concerning the daughters of Zelophehad: "They came to the entrance of the Tent of Meeting. They stood before Moses and Eleazar the priest and before the leaders and the congregation and said, "Our father died in the wilderness. He wasn't part of Korah's rebel anti-God gang. He died for his own sins. And he left no sons. But why should our father's name die out from his clan just because he had no sons? So give us an inheritance among our father's relatives." Numbers 27:2-4 (MSG)*

The enemy keeps back what belongs to us through false entitlement on the part of another. The daughters asked, *"Why should our fathers name die out from his clan just because he had no sons?"* No one had challenged this law of inheritance before now.

We too must challenge adversity by decreeing the promises of God. Let sickness, family strife, marital struggles, depression, fear, financial lack and all the things that come against us know that we're not having it. We must first know what our inheritance is and then petition God in prayer concerning His promise. We can't know what is legally ours if we don't read the contract. The bible is God's contract or covenant with us. I'm not saying we won't have opposition but that we don't have to make it feel at home when we have promises that contradict it.

For far too long only the sons were deemed worthy of their father's inheritance. The leaders presumed this law was fair in the eyes of God but they were dreadfully wrong.

The devil thinks that our children belong to him, but he is dreadfully wrong. He thinks our marriage belongs to him, but he is dreadfully wrong. He thinks our health, our wealth, businesses, career and our spiritual inheritance belong to him. But again, he is dreadfully wrong.

We must notify (by declaration of the word), the spirit of false entitlement - that its power is broken over our lives. Through the blood of Jesus, we have been made heirs of God's promises. Please note that the daughters did not primarily seek to demand their rightful inheritance - but instead to honor their fathers name and character. They sought to preserve his reputation before making their claim. The daughters of Zelophehad were not operating under the spirit of entitlement but were instead, seizing their rightful inheritance.

Our past does not determine our outcome in life.

Continuing in Numbers 27:2-4

- They declared their father's legal rights to an inheritance.
- They refuted all rights to withhold their father's inheritance from them.
- Once they successfully established their father's rights to an inheritance:
- They decreed it as their own.
- The daughters of Zelophehad said: *"Give us a possession among our father's brothers."*
- Moses brought their case before the Lord.
- *"The Lord said; the daughters of Zelophehad are right in their statement."*

The Message Bible goes on to tell us in verse 6:

> *"God ruled: "Zelophehad's daughters are right. Give them land as an inheritance among their father's relatives. Give them their father's inheritance."*

They were given the inheritance that would have been their fathers had he lived, and the Spirit of false entitlement was broken from over their lives that historic day.

A New Law was established

> *Verses 8-11 go on to say... "Then tell the People of Israel, If a man dies and leaves no son, give his inheritance to his daughter. If he has no daughter, give it to his brothers. If he has no brothers, give it to his father's brothers. If his father had no brothers, give it to the nearest relative so*

> that the inheritance stays in the family. This is the standard procedure for the People of Israel, as commanded by God through Moses."

This was not just a victory for the daughters of Zelophehad, but for all the daughters from this time forward.

> The daughters ask merely for "a possession among our father's brothers", However, God said concerning the death of a father leaving no sons but daughters from this time forward: "If a man dies and leaves no son, give his (whole) inheritance to his daughter…"

God exceeded the expectation of Zelophehad's daughters by not only granting them an inheritance and establishing a new law to include future daughters, but to give the fathers inheritance in its entirety, withholding nothing - If there were no daughters it would be passed down accordingly in order to keep it in the family.

The results of their perseverance against any and all obstacles were:

- They received their inheritance
- The father's name was no more disgraced because he had no sons, but only daughters
- A new law was imposed that included daughters to be given the 'whole' inheritance upon the death of a father when there are no sons

A Gateway of Hope
Chapter Nine

1). The Valley of Achor represents a place of deep trouble and despair. There God provides a door of hope.

> How have you seen God provide a door of hope in your valley of trouble or despair?

2). Gomer's name means *"Complete"*. She, like many of us, didn't know she was already complete.

> What were the consequences of Gomer not knowing she was already complete? How did it affect her and how can this apply to you?

3). Our future is secure in Christ.

> What concerns do you have about your future and how does this statement help you find peace?

4). We can learn lessons from our past.

> What transformative or life changing lessons have you learned from your past?

5). Gomer, driven by her pain, offered herself in search for significance.

> Can you identify with Gomer's pain or behavior and if so in what way?

Scriptural Inheritance Affirmation:

"I myself will tend my sheep and have them lie down, declares the Sovereign Lord. I will search for the lost and bring back the strays. I will bind up the injured and strengthen the weak…I will shepherd the flock with justice." Ezekiel 34: 15-16: (NIV)

CHAPTER TEN

A New Mindset

If not dealt with, the voice of fear seemingly merges with our own pattern of speaking and thinking. So much so, that we eventually assume that it is our own voice and fail to recognize its deception.

You can spend your entire life in preparation for destiny

We tend to think that walking in our destiny refers to standing in a pulpit, running revival meetings, holding crusades, speaking at conferences, performing concerts - and enjoying great success or ministering on a routine basis to multiple groups or audiences. Some see destiny as finding the love of our life or achieving a long-awaited dream or vision. While these are great accomplishments, if accomplished on our own, they can limit the plan of God for our lives. The actual definition of 'destiny' is: purpose, vocation, intention, calling, or future. Destiny is not always associated with ministry or corporate success alone. It covers every aspect concerning your life. It can be revealed in multiple ways. However destiny is revealed, and no matter how many destinations it takes before you reach your dreams, goals or visions – you will fulfill all that God has for you if you trust Him and submit to the process. Destiny simply refers to our destinations in life. It is as much about the journey as it is the finale. We may experience multiple excursions along the way. Some may be pleasure trips while others are detours and digressions. Some may be sudden, and others delayed. However, each venture works with the next in a sequence of pathways to destiny. We may meet destiny at various locations in life and in unexpected ways. A door might, without rhyme or reason, be opened to us or an opportunity presented that we did not anticipate simply because God willed it. We tend to esteem one experience above another judging from external appearances. If it meets a particular criterion, we think it is a manifestation of destiny. If it doesn't measure up or meet our benchmark, we decline and assume it is not from God. You've heard it said; *"all that glitters is not gold"*. Yes, we generally look for the glitter, assuming God is in it. On the contrary, destiny doesn't always show up in the obvious. It won't always come in an elegant package.

As seen in the daughters of Zelophehad and other great men and women of the Bible, destiny can require that you spend what seems like a life-time in preparation only to accomplish one great achievement that will influence or affect others for generations. At other times, it appears that appointments with destiny are spread intermittently throughout your life. Destiny can show up at various seasons of time. In other words, you may experience specific time frames for specific purpose, vocation, intention or calling as you progress into your future. As suddenly as a door opened, it can seem that it is now shut. Often the season can end as abruptly as it began.

Too many of us live by the *"what's in it for me mentality."* Our motive is to make a name for ourselves rather than lifting up the name of Jesus. Our hope is to gain self-recognition and vain glory. We are by nature, self-seeking and self-centered. As a result, we fail to live a life that is Christ-centered.

As followers of Christ, our ambition should be to leave an imprint on this world for Him by touching the lives of others with words of encouragement, support, hope and inspiration. Let's endeavor to lift one another and not walk over each other in an effort to elevate ourselves.

Like the daughters of Zelophehad, let's leave a story that can be told long after we're gone to stimulate others to hope.

You may be the only bible some people will read. Like the daughters of Zelophehad, allow your life to speak volumes through your actions.

We are His living epistles. Apostle Paul speaking to the church at Corinth said:

> *"Ye are our epistle (letters), written in our hearts, known and read of all men: Forasmuch as ye are manifestly declared to be the epistle (message) of Christ ministered by us, written not with ink, but with the Spirit of the living God; not in tables of stone, but in fleshy tables of the heart." 2 Corinthians 3:2-3 (KJV)*

We must seek to lift the fallen, strengthen the weak, heal the broken and restore the outcast to a position of inclusivity. Yes, we are our brother's keeper.

We do not have to be wealthy to achieve great success. We are wealthy when we successfully touch another life in a positive manner. When we inspire, encourage, edify or lift up another person, we are filled with the riches of joy that cannot come from any other source.

We walk past people every day who are hurting, beaten and broken, left for dead on the side of the road of life like the man in Luke 10:31:

> "A priest happened to be going down the same road, and when he saw the man, he passed by on the other side: So too, a Levite, when he came to the place and saw him, passed by on the other side. But a Samaritan, as he traveled, came where the man was; and when he saw him, he took pity on him. He went to him and bandaged his wounds, pouring on oil and wine. Then he put the man on his own donkey, brought him to an inn and took care of him." (NIV)

This man demonstrated love and compassion while the priest and the Levite (those supposedly representing God), crossed over to the other side of the road to avoid him.

We hear many stirring sermons and uplifting songs that touch our soul, but nothing speaks louder or touches us more deeply than the actions that flow from a heart of compassion toward one who is left wounded, battered and broken on the roadside of life.

Praise God for the good Samaritans. God uses those who are willing to step out of their comfort zone to make a difference in the life of another.

Your destiny is never about you, it is about walking out the will of God for your life to affect others.

You may have experienced deep distress in your life and think that God could never use someone who went through such dark despair. Take a look at the following scripture and think again.

> "You tried to harm me, but God made it turn out for the best, so that he could 'save' all these people, as he is now doing." Gen. 50:20 (CEV)

Your adversity is designed to turn out for not only your advantage, but the advantage of others as well. God will use your pain to minister hope, healing and deliverance to others. We not only sympathize (pity), with them in their pain, but we empathize (understand, identify) with them.

Opposition Can Be Our Friend

The daughters of Zelophehad suffered much opposition. God uses opposition to test and/or develop godly character in us so that we can later be entrusted to fulfill His desire for us and through us.

David speaking of Joseph said:

> "Until the time came to fulfill his dreams, the Lord tested Joseph's character." Psalm 105: 19 (NLT)

Joseph announced his dream to his family. But until the fulfillment of Joseph's word, The Lord 'tested' (tried, verified, confirmed, established and seasoned), his character.

God tells us to Fear No More...

The daughters of Zelophehad lost their natural father in the wilderness … but their Heavenly Father was still taking care of them. Zelophehad left an inheritance for his daughters, but they had to go after it. They had to pursue it by presenting their petition before Moses, the leaders, elders and the congregation. Despite the laws of the land and the culture of that day, they stepped out of their comfort zone. Also, Zelophehad left something better, stronger and more powerful than any physical inheritance. He taught them to trust God and believe in themselves. He left a legacy that we now read about that will continue to inspire and influence many for years to come.

Zelophehad stands as an example to fathers everywhere, showing them how a father does not have to succumb to his own fears or bondages. Godly fathers can escape the generational strongholds represented by their forefathers and break the power of the enemy from over their children.

A damaged father can become an over-comer and thus provide a secure environment for his family.

He does not have to have great wealth or extreme success to leave a legacy to his offspring.

The greatest riches a father can leave his children is having lived a Godly lifestyle before them and showing them what it means to have a personal relationship with Jesus Christ.

In him, his son's will learn how to be great husbands, fathers and leaders and his daughter's will learn what they must look for and expect in the man they marry.

Many people, because of fear, dishonor themselves by turning to ungodly lifestyles.

They pursue worldly vices to drown their fears and fill the emptiness within. Zelophehad did not allow fear to alter his character or diminish his morals. His past did not determine his ultimate destiny.

I am told that the brain responds to fear in various ways and sends messages to the body. The heart pounds and you break out in a sweat. The eyes dilate to allow you to see more. The body goes into fight or flight mode, you become tense, numbness can occur as well as dizziness and deep anxiety.

I had a fear of flying on airplanes. The thought of flying made me feel anxious. I missed an opportunity to go to Orlando, Florida to celebrate my youngest daughter's 30th birthday and later missed my son's wedding in Las Vegas because of that fear.

I was frustrated and very sorry I had missed these significant events in my children's lives. I was later invited to fly to Orlando again for vacation with a childhood friend. I struggled with the decision, but after much prayer, decided that I would no longer allow fear to control my life and hold me hostage. My husband prayed for me and I finally got a release. I made the flight arrangements. I still did not want to fly alone. So, I decided to travel several miles out of the way to catch a flight with my girlfriend. By the time I arrived at the airport, to my surprise, my fear turned to excitement. I found out that I had a window seat and I was like a little child in a candy shop. I pressed my face close to the window, enjoying the view all the way. I also had the privilege of sitting next to a young Youth Pastor and his lovely wife who kept me calm with comforting casual conversation. However, at one point they decided to put a movie into their personal DVD player. I love movies, but when I saw that they were looking at the movie *"Lost"*, (a story about a plane crash that left the passengers stranded on an island), I declined and decided to listen to gospel music on my iPod instead. I loved every minute! I couldn't get enough of this captivating new experience. I had been set free from the stronghold of fear. My only regret was that I had not defeated it sooner.

Power, Love and a Sound Mind

I want to elaborate for a moment on 2 Timothy 1:7 where it reads– *"For God has not given us a spirit of fear, but of power and of love and of a sound mind."* (NKJV)

There is a vast difference between walking in fear and walking in the powerful life of Christ on the inside of us.

The enemy uses fear to paralyze and intimidate us. God has given us as followers of Christ, the spirit of power and the spirit of love and the spirit of a sound (impregnable, impenetrable, invincible, secure) mind.

The spirit of 'Power' is by definition; control, influence, authority and rule.

The spirit of 'Love' by definition is; devotion, passion and also falls into the category of worship.

The spirit of a 'sound mind' by definition is a mind that is; undamaged, indestructible, positive, secure, sturdy and intact. It is having the mind of Christ or the mind of the Spirit.

Fear is the result of having a mind that is focused on self. When we put our mind on the things of God, our goal is to please him instead of appeasing our flesh.

Fear desires to ensnare you. It wants to entangle you in its web of deceit. Fear will entrap you, blind you and immobilize you. It is not in fear's nature to release you.

Fear can sometimes turn into severe phobias and the individual will begin to experience what is known as excessive fear.

Let's take a look at how fear affected men and women in the Bible and the result.

The Demoralization of fear: 1 Samuel: 13:5-8

"Now the Philistines gathered to fight against Israel, 30,000 chariots and 6,000 horsemen, and troops in multitude, like sand on the seashore. They came up and camped at Michmash, east of Beth-aven. When the men of Israel saw

> *that they were in a tight situation (for their troops were hard-pressed), they hid in caves, in thickets, in cellars, and in [dry] cisterns (pits)... As for Saul, he was still in Gilgal, and all the people followed him, trembling [in fear and anticipation]." (Amp. Bible)*

Fear comes to deflate you, depress you, discourage you and cause you to become disheartened. Fear desires to demoralize and traumatize you.

Fear's objective is to cause you to give up on life. Its desire is to discourage you and eventually drive you into deep depression.

These mighty men of God went into hiding because of fear. They got their eyes on the enemy and off of God.

The result: Fear will rob you of quality of life. You will alienate yourself and go into hiding. You feel diminished in life. These men were in a tight situation and went hiding in any whole big enough to contain them.

The Deprivation of Fear:

Fear aims to make you feel like you lack the ability to move forward in life. Your confidence is utterly destroyed. Its attempt is to deprive you of the experience of a full and satisfied life. You feel empty and depleted of any sense of joy and satisfaction.

> *Matt. 28:1-4 tells us: "...Mary Magdalene and the other Mary went to look at the tomb. There was a violent earthquake, for an angel of the LORD came down from heaven and, going to the tomb, rolled back the stone and sat on it. His appearance was like lightning, and his clothes were*

> *white as snow. The guards were so afraid of him that they shook and became like dead men."* (NIV)

The Result: You become anxious, shaken and become like dead men. You become estranged and uninterested. You lose concern for the things that you once enjoyed. This is right where the devil wants you.

The guards were anxious and trembled at the sight of the angel. When the angel spoke to the women, the guards could not engage in the conversation because of fear.

Fear kept them from hearing the good news about Jesus and His resurrection from the dead. It blinded their mind to the truth.

Fear will deprive you of the ability to advance in life. Fear will prevent you from functioning effectively. It will distort everything you see and hear and it will keep you from knowing the truth.

The Disturbance of Fear:

Fear causes chaos, torment, anxiety and confusion. A life of fear is filled with trouble, disorder and disruption.

> *In John 9:16-22 "They brought to the Pharisees the man who had been blind.... the Pharisees said, "This man is not from God..."*
> *.... So they were divided. Then they turned again to the blind man, "What have you to say about him? It was your eyes he opened." The man replied, "He is a prophet." They still did not believe...until they sent for the man's parents. "How is it that now he can see?" "We know he is our son," the parents answered, "and we know he was born blind". But how he can see now, or who opened his eyes, we don't*

know. Ask him. His parents said this because they were afraid of the Jewish leaders, who already had decided that anyone who acknowledged that Jesus was the Messiah would be put out of the synagogue. (NIV)

The Result: Fear will cause you to go along with a lie rather than stand on the side of truth concerning a matter. Fear challenges you to compromise your faith.

The Destination of Fear:

Fear has a starting point and an ending point. It does not give up until it reaches its destiny. It is fear's determination to ultimately meet its target and accomplish its goal to destroy you.

Fear is like sin; it will take you further than you wish to go and keep you longer than you wish to stay. Its ultimate destination is to keep you from reaching your highest potential. Fear has no place in the life of the believer. Fear wants to be the driving force in your life, but that would make fear lord and that position belongs only to Christ. Fear likes to dominate and be in control of an individual's life. Fear has traveling associates named terror, dread and horror. Terror causes panic and alarm; Dread causes anxiety and dismay and Horror causes disgust and repulsion.

They work together to cause self-loathing, lack of self-control, disappointment, worry, nervousness, concern and a host of other negative emotions that can ruin one's life.

Zelophehad gives us the remedy: He called out to God in prayer. We may not always know the exact words to use to describe how we feel, but God said that He knows every word on our tongue before we speak it. Our prayers do not have to be eloquent or elaborate. We can talk to God just like we would talk to a good friend.

Zelophehad also took time to listen to God. He didn't just pray a quick prayer and go back to his usual routine. He paused and spent time quietly before the Lord. We know this because he heard the counsel of God when He spoke to him. We think that God doesn't talk to us like that today or that He talks only to others. But the problem is we don't take the time to listen to Him. He may speak through His Word (the Bible), or a quiet whisper in your heart. He may even speak through a complete stranger. At any rate, you can rest assure that you will hear Him speak to you if you just listen. God will give you counsel (guidance, command, direction or warning).

When Zelophehad followed God's guidance, command, direction or warning, he and his daughters' lives were transformed.

Reflections

A New Mindset
Chapter Ten

1). The voice of fear merges with our own pattern of speaking/thinking and we assume it is our own.
> *How can we recognize the voice of fear?*

2). "Ye are our epistle (letter) …read of all men".
> *What does your life tell others about you?*

3). In what way(s) can opposition be your friend?
> *(Think about or discuss in group)*

4). The men of Israel hid themselves in caves, thickets, cellars and cisterns.
- *What has your response been when fear came knocking at your door?*
- *What was Zelophehad's remedy for fear?*

5). Has fear ever challenged you to compromise your faith?
> *In what way and what was the end result?*

Scriptural Inheritance Affirmation:

"When you go through deep waters and great trouble, I will be with you. When you go through rivers of difficulty, you will not drown! When you walk through the fire of oppression, you will not be burned up—the flames will not consume you." Isaiah 43:2 (TLB)

CHAPTER ELEVEN

Treasures of Darkness

> "I will go before you and make the hard places smooth. I will break the brass doors to pieces, and cut through their iron gates. I will give you riches hidden in the darkness and things of great worth that are hidden in secret places. Then you may know that it is I, the Lord, the God of Israel, who calls you by name."
>
> ISAIAH 45: 2-4 (NLV)

Before we reach our destiny, He is already there. Before we engage in the battle, He has already appointed the victory. Before we are aware that we have a need, He is already meeting it. He will smooth out the mountainous (high-places, surmounting struggles), and the hard (difficult, awkward, problematical or troublesome), places. He will break down every barrier and cut through every resistance. He will reveal the hidden (unknown, buried), treasures of darkness. He will unveil things of great worth or value previously shrouded (unseen, concealed), in the secret (undisclosed, whole-and-corner) places. Out of our darkest experiences come great treasures of resources, assets, riches and provisions. He said it is He, our Lord and God, who calls (summons, beckons) us by name.

You may be sitting in a very dark place in your life. Perhaps the enemy has you believing that it will never get better. Let me remind you that he (the enemy), is the father of all lies. Your secret places are about to open and give birth to hidden treasures and riches so vast, that you can hardly contain them. These are not necessarily treasures of silver, gold, or material wealth so much as it is treasures of personal growth and development, self-enrichment, spiritual enlightenment, emotional strength and stability. A deeper love for God and for the precious life He has given you is now realized. Your sense of value, significance and worth is heightened. Out of the dark places explodes the brilliance of who you are and the revealing of your maximum potential. Like the daughters of Zelophehad, you emerge with a greater understanding of your purpose and destiny. You come to realize that you are that hidden treasure.

Though seemingly placed upon a shelf, you are about to come into your own magnitude of distinction. The shelf was merely your incubation period as you evolved and matured into your new self. You were in preparation for the manifestation of the treasure that you are. Your darkness is transformed into a glorious, awe-inspiring, breathtaking light! Like the daughters of Zelophehad, the very thing that tried to hide you served to bring to light the treasure you were designed to be.

The whole community was watching the daughters of Zelophehad because he had no sons. Zelophehad had been ostracized and ridiculed. All eyes were on this family but it was a set-up.

Out of Darkness Comes Joyful Praise

We sometime find ourselves in a dark place of our own volition. God has something good to say about that too.

> *In Psalm 107:10-12 "Some sat in darkness and in the shadow of death. They suffered in prison in iron chains. 'Because they had turned against the Words of God. They hated what the Most High told them to do'. So He loaded them down with hard work. They fell and there was no one to help." (NLV)*

Yet in verse 13, it tells us concerning these same people:

> *"When they cried out to the Lord in their trouble, He saved them out of their distresses. He brought them out of darkness and the shadow of death, and broke their chains in pieces...He has broken the gates of bronze, and cut the bars of iron in two."*

Praise God! That's good news.

When Zelophehad called out to God, his whole world changed. His cry not only delivered him, but his daughters also. Once he and his daughters became free, a chain reaction took place. Women of future generations were delivered from the unjust law of inheritance. The leaders got free from their bias against women and began to see them differently. Cultural strongholds began to come down.

God brings us out of darkness so that we then become a light to those who are blind and taken captive. As a result, we get to be instrumental in bringing them out of their darkness.

Treasures in Earthen Vessels

In Second Corinthians 4:7 we read: "But we have this treasure in jars of clay to show that this all-surpassing power is from God and not from us..." (NIV)

Have you ever gone through a hard time only to realize that you possess greater treasures of strength, stamina, peace and joy on the inside of you that you could not have imagined? It is the darkness that reveals the light of Christ on the inside of us.

The following verse goes on to confirm that hidden treasures are unearthed during times of great distress.

Second Corinthians 4: 8-10: "We are hard pressed on every side, but not crushed; perplexed, but not in despair; persecuted, but not abandoned; struck down, but not destroyed.... so that the life of Jesus may also be revealed in our body." (NIV)

Our hearts are truly encouraged by the full assurance that results in our intimate relationship with Christ and the knowledge of His unconditional love. As we seek to know the Lord more and more, He makes these treasures known to us.

Our Identity is connected to our Destiny

The bible tells us that the thief comes to steal, kill and destroy. How does he do it? He steals our identity. If we do not know who we are in Christ Jesus, the enemy can sell us a bill of goods. He will tell us that we are nothing and nobody cares about us. He lies viciously and sows his seeds of negativity, doubt and fear. If we believe him, we will never be able to obtain the promises of God. We will have poor health, poor relationships and poor attitudes and never reach our destiny. He uses people in authority to speak negative things over us as children. He uses bullies to verbally, emotionally and physically attack us during childhood. He'll even use family members and friends to say hurtful things, sometime, unknowingly or unintentionally.

> Ps. 147: 3 *"He heals the brokenhearted and binds up their wounds [curing their pains and their sorrows]." (Amplified Version)*

Contrary to popular belief, what we don't know can and will hurt us.

Like Zelophehad and his first two daughters, struggling under the shadow of fear, I didn't know of God's acceptance and approval. I didn't know that He formed me with a purpose in mind. I didn't know that I was a daughter of the Most High God. I didn't know that God knew me before I was formed in my mother's womb and neither did I realize that He loves me with an everlasting, unconditional love. I didn't know that He had a plan for my life to prosper me and to give me a future and a hope. I didn't know that I was the apple of His eye, that I am tattooed on the palm of His hand. I didn't know that I had such a wonderful savior, healer, redeemer, deliverer…I didn't know that He sings over me with joy and dances over me with rejoicing. I didn't know that He is for me and not against me…I didn't know… And what I didn't know was hurting me.

When I cried out to God, I began to understand that I am who God says I am. I can do what He says I can do and can have what He says I can have. It's time we take back our identity and believe what God says in His word about us.

I referred to a particular scripture earlier that I want to repeat here using The Message Bible:

Psalm 139: 13 – 18:

> "Oh yes, you shaped me first inside, then out; you formed me in my mother's womb. I thank you, High God - you're breathtaking! Body and soul, I am marvelously made! I worship in adoration – what a creation! You know me inside and out; you know every bone in my body; You know exactly how I was made, bit by bit, how I was sculpted from nothing into something. Like an open book, you watched me grow from conception to birth; 'all the stages of my life were spread out before you, the days of my life all prepared before I'd even lived one day'. Your thoughts – how rare, how beautiful! God, I'll never comprehend them! I couldn't even begin to count them- any more than I could count the sand of the sea."

Our destiny or destination in life was written before our conception. We are on a journey; our purpose, aim, goal, objective and intention are already determined by our Heavenly Father. We can get there on target or by delay like the Israelites in the wilderness - depending on our response to life's interruptions and distractions or if we keep our eyes on the Lord.

Our identity is so connected to our destiny, that what we believe about our self in terms of significance and self-worth, will either obstruct or accelerate our destiny. How we respond when being tested will either hinder or hasten our end result. Your life's story is already written. We were sculpted 'from nothing into something'. And, like an open book, the days of our lives were spread out. He watched us 'from conception to birth'. All the stages of our life were 'prepared before we'd even lived one day'. Wow! It is an overwhelming reality to comprehend the fullness of Gods preparedness for our lives.

As a man thinks or imagines in his heart (mind), so is he. When we change our thoughts, we change our lives. In so doing, we secure our identity and reclaim our future.

When we resist worry and anxiety, peace will act as a guardrail around our minds - and we will not lose control and go over the edge like a speeding car on a slippery slope that ends up in a ravine.

Our thoughts change the course of our life

The daughters of Zelophehad were on their way to becoming the daughters of *"Shadow of Fear"*, but Zelophehad changed their course of life when he called out to God. His new perspective transformed him from a man of fear to a man of faith.

He set the stage for his family and turned the direction of his daughters. They went from being the *"Daughters of The Shadow of Fear"* to *"Daughters of Destiny."*

With fear gone, they had the power to be all that God had designed them to be and to do all He had intended for them to accomplish. Nothing could stop them; nothing could hold them back and nothing could keep them down.

Perhaps you have thought patterns that you know need to be modified or adjusted if you wish to reach your destiny. If we 'think we can' do a thing, then we will, but if we 'think we can't', then we won't. Our thoughts are the force that will either push us forward or stop us in our tracks. The way we think can be our greatest advantage or our worse shortcoming. We must therefore, examine every thought and determine its origin. Where did that thought come from? If it is not true, noble, pure, and lovely or of a good report then it is not a godly thought. If there is no virtue (good advantage), or if it is not praiseworthy (creditable or good), Philippians 4: 8 tells us to get rid of it. Don't dwell on or entertain it.

Reflections

Treasures of Darkness
Chapter Eleven

"Out from Darkness comes Joyful Praise."

1). In Psalms 107: 10-12 we read how some sat in darkness because, in frustration, they turned against Gods word. Yet, when these same people cried out to God, He saved them out of their distresses.
> *Can you think of a time when in frustration the same thing happened to you?*

2). We read about hidden treasures:

- *What hidden treasures have tests and trial revealed in your life?*
- *On the contrary, how have you experienced the unearthing of hidden treasures arising from your relationship with Christ?*

3). "What we don't know, can hurt us."
> *As you've matured in your relationship with Christ can you now look back and identify areas that you struggled in simply because of your initial lack of knowledge of who God is?*

4). Review Psalms 139: 13-18: How does this passage speak to you?
(Think about or discuss in group)

5). *"Our thoughts change the course of our lives."*
Are you aware of any thoughts that you know you need to take control over?

Scriptural Inheritance Affirmation:

"Turn my way, look kindly on me, as you always do to those who personally love you. Steady my steps with your Word of promise so nothing malign gets the better of me. Rescue me from the grip of bad men and women so I can live life your way. Smile on me, your servant; teach me the right way to live. I cry rivers of tears because nobody's living by your book!" Psalm 119: 132-136 (MSG)

CHAPTER TWELVE

Living Your Legacy

Refuse to allow your past, present circumstances, foolish choices or other negative experiences define you.

Now that we have gleamed from the story of Zelophehad and his family, what do we learn from their experience? How do we apply this knowledge and grow from it?

It is time for us to live our legacy. Claim our inheritance and take ownership of our God given birthright.

Don't live under the umbrella of your past. Come out of the land of what was and live in the joy of what is. Refuse to allow your negative past to dictate your future. Recognize that your destiny is in the hands of God, but it takes you working in concert with Him to fulfill it.

Know that even though things do not always go as you plan, God has a plan specifically for you. His plans for you began before you were knitted together in your mother's womb. His plan is always for your good. The things the enemy means for evil, God will turn for your favor and His Glory. He will cause all things to work together for your ultimate advantage.

Be prepared to allow God to use you in whatever situation you find yourself.

Look for the best in others. We all have flaws and imperfections, but we also have individual gifts, talents, skills and contributions to make in this life. Stir up the gifts inside you through spending intimate time with the Lord in prayer. Your life is valuable, precious and significant. It is filled with purpose.

Let God continue to perform a good and perfect work in you. We are not our own. We have been purchased by the blood of Jesus and God has regained ownership of us through the death, burial, resurrection and ascension of His Son. His timing may not be our timing, but His timing is perfect. His ways may not be our ways, but His ways are for our higher good.

Never belittle the power and plan of God for your life.

Remember that love requires that we look beyond the faults of others and see their needs. Let's not go around devouring one another. Love never gives up, fades or quits. Love always believes the best about a person. Take every opportunity to advance someone else.

We must also learn to love ourselves in the same manner and not be hypercritical with ourselves. Don't be overly judgmental of yourself. See others and yourself through the eyes of our Heavenly Father.

Silence the internal critic and learn to speak words of affirmation over yourself.

Lay aside every weight, every burden and every care. They will only hinder your race. Cast them all at the feet of Jesus.

Cultivate the soil of your heart. Nurture, encourage, develop and foster a heart of readiness to receive the word of God. Develop a mindset to apply the things you learn from His word. Stop worrying with excess. Worry will choke out the word of God in your heart and cause you to walk in darkness.

Darkness produces fear. Refuse to allow fear to dominate your life.

God's word is a lamp unto your feet and a light unto your path. The footsteps of the righteous man or woman are ordered by the Lord. The path of the righteous grows brighter and brighter day by day.

Make Christ the head of your life. He will turn your sorrow to joy, grieving to laughter and restore what the enemy has stolen from you. Trust Him unconditionally!

He will give you Songs of Praise and Shouts of Deliverance

It's time you get your song back, get your joy back, and get your peace back. Feel the dance of rejoicing in your feet again. Call out to God! He is waiting. Pour yourself out before Him like water.

He knows your frame.

As a Father pities his children, so the Lord pities those who reverence Him.

As we continue to develop an intimate relationship with Jesus Christ through prayer, worship and the reading of His word, we begin to experience greater and greater freedom from our past hurts, disappointments, pain and shame. We learn that He has cast our sins into the sea of forgetfulness as far as the east is from the west.

We understand that He knows our frame (he knows how we are built, the stuff we are made of). As an earthly father strives to be compassionate, sympathetic and merciful toward his children, God too is kind and tenderhearted toward those who fear (reverence, respect and honor) Him. He remembers that we are but dust.

(Ps. 103:12-13). The Lord is our hiding place. He promises to preserve us from trouble. He delivers us from the disgrace of our past and gives us victory over fear.

Like Zelophehad, we must call out to Him and receive His counsel. He tells us in Psalm 32: 8

"I [the Lord] will instruct you and teach you in the way you should go; I will counsel you with My eye upon you." (AMPC)

The daughters of Zelophehad went from fear to fame, from distress to destiny and from the uncertainty of their future to discovering a glorious future and a hope.

As a child of God, you walk in complete forgiveness of sin. You are free from guilt and shame. Great waters of trial may overflow you but they will not touch your spirit. He promises to encompass you with mercy and loving kindness. As you walk in these you will continue to discover your identity and your destiny.

Know That God Uses Average People

Remember, the daughters of Zelophehad (born under a shadow of fear) initiated a change to the laws of inheritance that would include daughters in future transactions and affecting the future of every daughter born to a father who had no sons upon his death. You too can initiate change that will affect your life and the future of others.

Fear tried to define the daughters of Zelophehad but instead they defied fear. They denied its power over them. You can do the same thing. The daughters of Zelophehad used their unique personalities and their average voices to collectively change their destiny. You can use your voice to declare a future blessed beyond expectation. Call yourself free, victorious, overcomer, and champion of the faith. See yourself fulfilling the dreams and visions that are in your heart. Imagine yourself accomplishing the goals and aspirations that you have set before you. God is able to transform your life to the point where you will be hardly recognizable to those who know you.

Favor Surrounds You like a Shield

Fear lost its grip and the voice of the daughters of Zelophehad was not only heard before the people, but the God of heaven and earth confirmed their request and it was awarded to them. God gave them favor with those in authority. Their lives were transformed forever and their fame went throughout the world.

When referring to the past, we think about something that happened many years ago, conceivably something in our childhood, teenage years or as an early adult. In reality, the past includes something as recent as that thing that happened yesterday or as little as an hour ago. We can't change what has already happened or what we've done, what we've said, or what we've experienced. We can however, change its power to influence, control, manipulate, dominate, rule or dictate our expectation.

Your past is behind you!

When something is behind us, it has a tendency to try to push us. I don't like how it makes me feel when someone is driving closely behind me on the highway at an accelerated speed. It feels as if they are riding my bumper and as if they want to push me out of their way. I find this very disturbing. That is how our past is. It feels like it is right behind us, riding our bumper and trying to force us onto the side of the road of life or to go into a wrong direction or to make a rash decision based on our emotions or our fear. If we allow the past to terrorize us, our past will have a collision with our present resulting in a potential fatality to our future.

We are not victims to our past. It cannot and will not hold us hostage. We are victors through Christ. He calls us more than a conqueror.

Refuse to allow your past to determine your destiny. It's time we take back the power we have relinquished to our past mistakes, mishaps and misfortunes and live life more completely and deliberately. We must believe that God has something better for us and that it is just around the corner. Some of us already have a great life but cannot enjoy it because our eyes are reflecting on our past instead of living in the present.

It's time we live life with expectation of good and not of doom and gloom. See yourself as a victor and not a victim of your past. Refuse to allow your past to determine your outcome.

We can't change the past but we can change our perception of it.

> *We read in Philippians 3:13, "I do not consider, brethren, that I have captured and made it my own [yet]; but one thing I do [it is my one aspiration]: forgetting what lies behind and straining forward to what lies ahead ..." (Amp. Bible)*

We must make the pursuit of freedom from the past our one aspiration. Our negative past leaves us feeling like we've lost out on something, but if we would be honest with ourselves, it is usually the hardships, sufferings and losses of our past that lead us to Christ. Those very things that were meant to destroy us; out of desperation they became the compelling force that pushed us toward Christ. It was when I felt that I had nothing left to live for that I decided to turn what remained of my life over to Christ. I knew that I had nothing to lose and everything to gain.

We must count them (the things of our past), as rubbish! Make a conscious choice today to take those things that the enemy meant to block us and allow God to turn them into conduits of victory. Out of our intimate relationship with Christ comes the release of His glorious resurrection power to restore to life all of our dead dreams, hopes, desires, potential, aspirations and ambitions.

We can't alter our history, but we can strip it of its power to influence us negatively by changing how we perceive it. Stop viewing it as something dreadful and shameful. Instead, see it as the very catapult that thrusts you into your destiny.

See it as an experience that made you better, stronger, and wiser. When we change how we view our past, everything around us will change.

It does not matter where you begin in life but where you end.

Continue to submit your life to Christ daily. He promises that He will perfect (finalize, complete) that which concerns you.
Spend time in prayer each day. Read the bible daily. Begin with the four gospels (Matthew, Mark, Luke and John). You will get to know more about Christ from these readings. Build new relationships with people who share your faith.

Should you fall, get back up and continue on your new journey with Christ. Remember, He loves you. He is a forgiving God. His mercies are new every morning and His compassions toward us are never failing.

God is the author and finisher of your faith. He will take opposing circumstances that you face and cause them too ultimately work for you and not against you.

Your past does not determine your destiny. Your current circumstances do not dictate your future. Your present does not define you. Keep moving forward!

When we live life looking through the lens or scope of fear, it distorts our view. We can't fully celebrate the present because we live perpetually in the past. The joys of new and vibrant relationships are tainted by the memory of painful past relationships. We refuse to trust for fear of betrayal. Great potentials are lost because we fail to try. Doors to new opportunities are closed because we are afraid to walk through them. Exciting experiences are refused because we feel incapable. We curse our future by holding onto various pains, letdowns, and frustrations. By doing this, we subconsciously set ourselves up to replicate the same past results.

We must learn to let go of our fears and embrace the hope of a better future by discovering the promises of our new inheritance through Christ. Be free from the dis-ease that fear has produced and be healed. Expect to move forward effortlessly into the new things that lie ahead. Let go of the trembling, unsteady and apprehensive emotions and live fearlessly.

Your eulogy has not been preached. Live your life entirely and purposefully.

God has brought you out of darkness and into His glorious light.

Our past does not define (describe, express, or characterize) us. Our life story is still being written on this side of heaven. Live life one chapter, one page, and sometime one paragraph or sentence at a time.

Now that you understand that each destination, each bend in the road of life takes you into your ultimate purpose, intent or future, realize that even now, you are standing at destiny's threshold. You are on the verge of the dawning of a new day. Whenever you are faced with a decision (a choice, resolution or assessment), you are at the threshold of destiny. Evaluate your options prayerfully. Consider seeking counsel from trusted advisers. Refuse to rush to judgement or a conclusion. Expect that every experience is working in your favor to bring you into a new level of confidence, trust and development. Close the door of the past and step over the doorsill before you. Enter into the destiny predetermined by God before your conception that awaits you. A new day is emerging. Believe it and receive it. I say again, Your History does not determine your destiny. Your past does not dictate your future. Your current circumstances do not control your outcome in life.

Wear Your Crown

I want to leave you with this thought. Believe that your best years are ahead of you. As you pursue your dreams, follow your passions and claim your destiny, remember that before you were created for destiny, you were created for God. He created you for Himself. He desires that your relationship with Him precede your relationship with the pursuit of destiny. If we put the pursuit of dreams, passions and destiny before Him then our priorities are miss-aligned. Don't make destiny an idol. Seek God first and all these things will come into place in His time, in His way and in His season. Be God driven, seeking how you may please and serve Him above all else. Take the next step and crossover the threshold. Leave the subsequent steps to God. As you do so, take a moment to breathe in and exhale. Breathe out all the toxins of your past. Release the yokes of oppression, doubt and fear. Discard any excess baggage from former negative relationships. Abandon cares about what others may think of you. Leave your past behind. Rise above your circumstances. You are called to *"Excel"*, which means: be excellent · be brilliant · be outstanding · be skillful · be proficient · be confident · be secure · reign supreme · wear the crown.

Like the daughter's of Zelophehad, step over the threshold of destiny. Seize your inheritance and fulfill your purpose. Excellence lies within you. You are empowered, qualified and thoroughly equipped.

Reflections

Living Your Legacy
Chapter Twelve

Reflect on the following statements: Think about them or discuss them in group.

- *Refuse to allow your negative past to dictate your future.*

- *Cultivate the soil of your heart.*

- *Use your voice to declare a future blessed beyond belief.*

- *Your past is behind you. Don't allow it to push you off destiny's path.*

- *We can't change the past but we can change our perception of it.*

- *It does not matter where you begin, but where you end.*

- *Believe that your best years are ahead of you.*

- *Follow your passions and claim your destiny.*

- *Don't make "destiny" an idol.*

- *Don't be destiny driven, be God driven.*

- *You are not a victim of past mistakes, bad choices, and inappropriate behavior – you are part of God's Master Plan.*

Scriptural Inheritance Affirmation:

"May the Lord answer you in the day of trouble; May the name of the God of Jacob defend you; May He send you help from the sanctuary, And strengthen you...May He grant you according to your heart's desire, And fulfill all your purpose...May the Lord fulfill all your petitions." Psalm 20: 1-5 (NKJ)

Practical Application Page

Now that you've read about the daughters of Zelophehad and the wonderful transformation resulting from crying out to God and following His counsel – let's put what we've learned into action.

This page is designed to provide specific life changing principles. Transformation comes gradually and with persevering practice. I encourage you to read the following 12 Power Principle Points and adopt them as your daily affirmation until you get them in your spirit. Each starts with the letter "R" to help you remember the ones most relevant to you. What you confess, you will possess. As you meditate and confess these principles - the words that come out of your mouth will go into your ears then down into your heart. Finally, as you think in your heart so shall you be. The results will be life altering. My heartfelt prayers are with you as you go from Standing at the Threshold of your Destiny to literally stepping over into all that God has for you. Put your anxieties behind and take the next step.

- Realize your past is behind you and leave it there.

- Recognize and cast down negative thoughts, imaginations and self-talk.

- Remember that your identity is in Christ.

- Refuse to allow your past to define you.

- Rehearse positive affirmations and declarations over your life routinely.

- Refrain from ungodly relationships, soul ties and influences.

- Reference biblical scriptures that speak to your heart and meditate on them.

- Run hard after God. Pursue Him with a passion. Make Him your priority.

- Reconcile with your past. Make peace with it by forgiving yourself and others.

- Release all sense of guilt, shame and condemnation by giving them to the Lord.

- Resist comparing yourself to others and enjoy your authentic uniqueness.

- Repeat: *"My identity is found solely in Christ; I am defined by who He says I am. My history does not determine my destiny – my past does not dictate my future; my present does not control my outcome in life. Past hurts, pains or failures no longer characterize me. I am standing at the threshold of my destiny. Before me lies an incredible future."*

Rejoice & Live Your Life Intentionally (Purposefully, Deliberately, By Design).

You Are Standing at the Threshold. Take the next step. Your Destiny awaits!

Make Christ your Life Coach

When Zelophehad called out to God, God became his life coach. God made him a champion of faith. God provided wisdom, insight and direction. He gave Zelophehad the enthusiasm, fortitude and tenacity to break free from fears stronghold.

As you submit more and more to the Lordship of Christ, transformation is inevitable. The more we learn of Him and discover His unconditional love for us, the more we experience conversion. A transfiguration takes place and we began to look to our future with hope, excitement and expectation. We will emerge into a new and glorious aftereffect like the caterpillar emerges into a butterfly.

We will never forget fully the things of our opposing past, but when we look back, we will no longer feel the shame, pain, hurt, disappointment or fear. We can look back and say: *"Look what the Lord has done"*! He changes our mourning into dancing.

Your past has no power to limit, hinder or restrain you. You are a child of the Most High God and if He be for you, who or what can be against you. You are an overcomer! You struggle successfully against difficulties and disadvantages. You come out a winner every time. You are not a victim of past mistakes, bad choices or inappropriate behavior. You are a new creation in Christ Jesus! God sent His son to make you free and who the Son sets free, is free in deed. Be not entangled again with the yoke of bondage but walk in your new-found freedom from fear and the influence of your past.

> *Gal. 5:1 "Stand fast therefore in the liberty by which Christ has made us free, and do not be entangled again with a yoke of bondage." (NKJV)*

I don't want you to miss out on the blessings that are in store for you through Jesus Christ. Having a personal relationship with Him is the greatest joy one can ever know.

> *John 3:16 tells us: "For God loved the world so much that he gave his only Son so that anyone who believes in him shall not perish but have eternal life." (NLB)*

If you have never invited Christ into your heart, now is the time to consider doing so. Simply pray this prayer.

> *"Father, I confess that I am a sinner. I ask you to forgive me of all my sins. Come into my heart and live in me. Remove all that is not pleasing to you and make me your own. I believe that Jesus is the Son of God and that He died for me, taking my sins upon Himself so that I might stand before You just as if I've never sinned. I confess that Jesus Christ is Lord of my life and renounce all other gods, thank you Lord for saving me, In Jesus Name. Amen"*

Congratulations! I encourage you to pray and find a church where you can connect and grow in your new-found faith.

ADDITIONAL RESOURCES:

New American Standard Bible
(1960, 1962, 1963, 1968, 1971, 1971. 1973, 1975, 1977)
(Definition of names)

Microsoft Thesaurus
(Word definitions and synonyms')

Bible Gateway (Searchable on-line Bible)
(Search of Various Bible Versions)

About the Author

Rev. Helen Hopkins is an extraordinary teacher of the word of God. She resides in Wilmington, Delaware with her husband of 39 years, Stanford Hopkins. Together they hosted a local television ministry program, *"Touching You"*, for several years. Helen speaks at conferences, seminars and workshops where she edifies, strengthens, encourages, and ministers hope and healing to the broken. Helen is a 1995 graduate of the Victory Christian Fellowship School of Biblical Studies in New Castle, Delaware where she earned a Diploma, and Ministerial license. At the same time, she established and led a local women's ministry where she developed leadership, mentored and provided spiritual support. She has served as worship leader, soloist and concert artiste. Helen attends Love of Christ Church where she has also served as small group leader, coach, prayer minister and urgent prayer request coordinator.

You can contact Rev. Helen through email:
StandingAtTheThreshold2019@gmail.com

mpliance